WILD TONGUES
CAN'T BE
TAMED

WILD TONGUES CAN'T BE TAMED

15 Voices from the Latinx Diaspora

....

Edited by

SARACIEA J. FENNELL

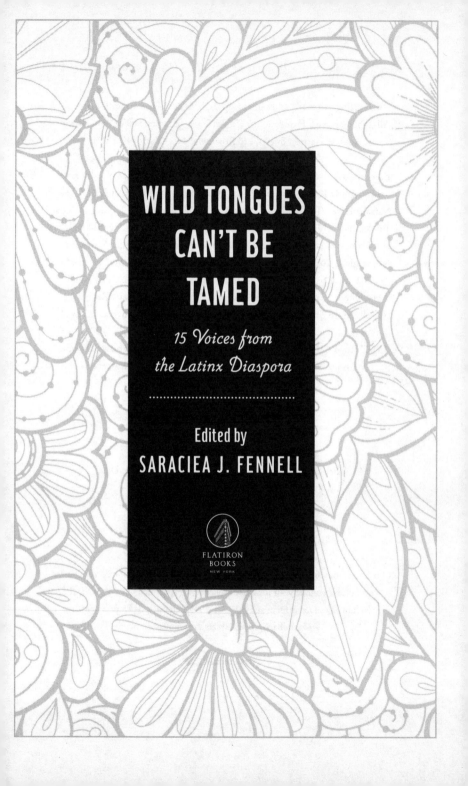

FLATIRON
BOOKS
NEW YORK

www.flatironbooks.com

Designed by Michelle McMillian

The Library of Congress Cataloging-in-Publication Data
is available upon request.

ISBN 978-1-250-76342-6 (hardcover)
ISBN 978-1-250-76341-9 (ebook)

Our books may be purchased in bulk for promotional, educational, or business
use. Please contact your local bookseller or the Macmillan Corporate and
Premium Sales Department at 1-800-221-7945, extension 5442, or by email at
MacmillanSpecialMarkets@macmillan.com.

First Edition: 2021

10 9 8 7 6 5 4 3 2 1

FOR MY FAMILY,
AND ALL CHILDREN OF THE DIASPORA

Contents

Introduction

I am so excited to share this anthology with the world. Too often individuals from the Latinx diaspora are placed into a box, into stereotypes, that society deems necessary in order to define us. But we are so much more than the myths, than the stereotypes, than what white people and Western ideals, want us to believe. So much gratitude to writers and activists who have come before me, like Gloria Anzaldúa, whose very book, *Boderlands/La Frontera*, served as inspiration for this one and from which the title was drawn—mil gracias. It was important to me to uplift and share voices from the Latinx diaspora from some of the most powerful writers that I personally admire. Some of these writers might be new to you, and others might seem like old favorites, but each of their essays packs a punch and shoots through the veil of what folks think they know about the Latinx experience. These writers don't hold back their opinions, their experiences, or their truths—there's no biting of the tongue or performative niceties here. Instead, we are letting our truths run wild, and pushing against whatever it is you think is the ideal Latinx individual. I hope you read with an open mind, and think critically about the topics discussed. More importantly, to the children of the diaspora, I hope you feel seen, and always know that you matter—no matter what the world tries to tell you.

Con cariño,
Saraciea

Write with your eyes like painters, with your ears like musicians, with your feet like dancers. You are the truthsayer with quill and torch. Write with your tongues of fire.

—GLORIA ANZALDÚA

WILD TONGUES
CAN'T BE
TAMED

Eres Un Pocho
Mark Oshiro

Eres un pocho.

You are seven.

They will ask you many questions. Why is your hair like that? Why are your eyes so dark? Are you a demon? How come you are so tan? There are no beaches in Idaho!

You will assure them every time that you are just like them.

You will look in the mirror and know you are not.

Your teacher will point to places on a map, one with borders drawn in black, countries and states filled with bright colors, and she will point below your country to another, and when she asks your class what it is, a young white girl will point at you. You will tell them you are not Mexico.

(You say this out of disbelief. But you will later know that this is the first time you associate shame with this thing you don't understand.)

They will stare back, eyes wide, foreheads crinkled in confusion, and your teacher will say, "When was the last time you ate a taco?"

You have never had one.

(Not a real one, at least. You know the ones at Taco John's are bland, without seasoning, without heart.)

You say nothing.

You will disappear into yourself.

Eres un pocho.

You are eight.

You are outside Adelanto, a town you've never been to before, one you will later pass on the highway twenty years later and recall this memory all over again. Your whole life has been uprooted, and what few friends you had will fade away. Years later, you will be unable to recall their names. You have been in the van for hours, your bladder full. Mom has barked at you enough times that you have learned how to ignore the pain down below. You are used to not being believed.

There is snow on the distant mountains. You don't know if this is the last time you'll see it. (It's not.) You've been told that where you are headed is hot. Arid. Dry. It is nothing like Boise. You will later learn just how true this is.

The hotel is small and smells of age and antiseptic. You are carted to a restaurant nearby that promises authentic Mexican cuisine. You wonder if it is anything like the bland imitations you have eaten before.

The staring starts almost immediately and you are used to it. You have adapted to what happens when you walk into any space with your family. People will glance from you to your parents and back, then to your blond, green-eyed sister, then back to you and your twin. You have years of experience with the dismay that crosses their faces—you know what it is like to have someone look at you and communicate a simple message:

You do not make sense.

You have known you were adopted for a long time. There was no way to hide it: a white mother and a dark-skinned Japanese father born in Hawaii. You never even got to be curious about it. You were told early, and you made it part of who you were. But you learn not long after that first conversation that *knowing* you are adopted does not help other people understand you. So you will become used to the odd expressions on the faces of strangers, the way that people will make you feel like an anomaly, like an exhibit in a zoo.

That does not happen this time. As the waitress brings out a hot plate piled with yellow rice, steaming and flavorful, the grains spilling over into the dark brown frijoles, she lingers. Her hair is dark like yours. Her eyes are dark like yours. You have never seen anyone else like this before.

(Only when looking at your twin or in the mirror.)

(This is often not enough.)

She stares at you and your brother. Then at your parents, one pale, the other dark, then glances back at you.

And then when she makes eye contact, she hits you with it, something you won't understand for years, but when you do, so much of your childhood will make sense.

It's pity. She wears it on her face as she leaves, and you scoop up some of the frijoles into your mouth, and they taste nothing like you've had before. You are savoring this experience when you look up and see the waitress. She points in your general direction.

No, you realize, that isn't quite right.

She is pointing you out to the cook.

The one who also looks like you.

He shakes his head. You won't understand this for a while.

You just eat.

It is delicious.

You will be surrounded by people who look like you soon. It will overwhelm you. It will be like a piece of the puzzle that is your sense of self falling into place. Just one piece, though. You still need many others.

You will see it as a blessing.

Your mother will see it as a curse.

Eres un pocho.

You are nine.

Those words are uttered all the time. You ask what they mean. No one will tell you. The kids who surround you, who speak Spanish rapidly and proudly, will titter and giggle and refuse to answer. "¡Eres un pocho!" they cry. They laugh. They run away from you. No one wants to be your friend.

You don't know what that word is.

You just know it hurts.

You will turn in a spelling quiz.

You will get it handed back.

She will put it face down on your desk.

Smile.

And say:

"I didn't expect you to be so smart!"

The corners of her mouth will upturn in what she thinks is a smile.

You know—even back then—that it is a slap in the face.

Eres un pocho.

You are twelve.

Middle school often feels like a waking nightmare. You are outgrowing your clothes, but your mother will refuse to buy you anything new. She will tell you it is because of money. That is probably true—your family has never had much of it. But it is also because the current style of dress in your school involves baggy, oversized clothing. As your jeans become tighter and tighter, the kids around you will turn on you.

You should ignore them. They are just as messed up, unsure, and afraid as you are.

But you won't. There is a boy, though. Carlos. You will later realize that he is the first person you will fall for. It is not love—that won't happen for a long time. Love can't exist without reciprocity. While you two will strike up a friendship over music, he will later betray you, too, when Kelly breaks up with you after a week. She will tell everyone she had to because you're gay.

You don't have the courage (yet) to own that truth. Instead, the truth is only another thing that sets you apart.

Before that happens, though, Carlos rips a split for you. He hands you a cassette at lunch. Los Crudos and Manumission. Five songs. You hide it under your mattress as if it is illicit material.

(In your house, it is.)

You check out a Spanish dictionary from your junior high library.

You start learning. So many things begin to make sense, to have a clarity they did not before.

You practice the words at home, late at night, while the lights are out and your parents think you are asleep. You cannot seem to roll your *R*'s, at least not the first hundred times or so. It is as if your tongue is made of lead, as if someone has cast it in iron.

(Someone has. Some*thing* has. You won't know what just yet.)

(Hold on.)

You start to ask questions at home. Who were your parents? Why don't we talk about them?

You will not get any answers.

Ever.

Eres un pocho.

They will still call you this.

You still won't get it.

(Soon.)

Even though you know what it literally means: you gave up your culture. You assimilated. You threw away everything so that you could fit in here, in a country that wants monotony. You try to explain that you didn't give up anything, that it was *taken* from you, but this doesn't matter to them. You betrayed who you were.

You will try. Because that's what you do: You try harder than anyone. People notice this, not always in the best light.

You will not fit in.

(Yet.)

You will keep trying.

Eres un pocho.

You are fifteen.

You have two years of high school Spanish under your belt. It is helping. You are not where you wish you were, but there are so many things you understand now. You can respond when you need to. Your mouth sometimes cannot move quickly enough—your brain still stumbles because conjugations are not natural to you. But there is a new way people look at you when these new words come out of your mouth.

Eyes go wide.

(It is shock.)

Mouths drop open slightly.

(Still shock.)

A lightness.

(Sometimes: relief. Sometimes: pride. Sometimes: dismissal.)

(You won't always know which it is.)

Yet at home, you are met with only one reaction: you are changing for the worse. You are ruining your life. You are guaranteeing only one thing: failure.

But most of these things are said only to *you*. There is no iteration of it forced upon your younger sister, who has pale skin and green eyes and blonde-brown hair. You will watch her get everything you once asked for and were denied; you will witness her being granted freedoms and responsibilities that are never offered to you. Your brother will bear some of the same as you, but only up to a point. He plays football. His wrist doesn't hang when he speaks. He has had a girlfriend for years. Only part of him is unacceptable, but it seems sometimes, your mother is willing to look past this because the rest of him . . . the rest of him is *right*.

You will know at the time that this is wrong. You will have none of the words, none of the concepts, none of the tools to dismantle this. You will simply tell your mother that there's nothing wrong with

speaking another language,

combing your hair a certain way,

listening to music you love,

being

(brown)

(queer)

(your true self).

You wish you could say *those* things aloud.

You don't.

Yet.

Eres un pocho.

You are sixteen.

You will make a choice. It will seem revolutionary at the time because your mother has tried to teach you that there is no greater scourge on the earth than the Catholic Church. She has tried to get you to believe that they are all going to Hell. You have noticed that she didn't start saying this until you moved to California, until she saw all the churches with their signs advertising mass in Spanish. And so, when she rejects you, when she finally wishes you weren't around, you take her up on her word, and you leave.

You have never been more alone. You feel cast out by the very person who made you feel so invisible, so confused, and you will wonder if you will ever find your place in the world.

Then it happens. It will seem like the most sensible thing in the world. Your friend—who will later become your godparent—will ask you if you need help. You will say yes. He will take you in, introduce you to his family, and then introduce you to a community.

All with brown skin.

All with dark hair.

All with dark eyes.

They look at you with love and adoration and kindness.

You will not understand for two years that this is not what is in their eyes.

But for the moment, you join their church. They are Catholics, and they seem so loving. Accepting. Eager to have you as part of their family. You go to mass for the first time. It is entirely in Spanish. You are spoken to in a language you still only have a rudimentary grasp on, but you believe you are up for the challenge.

You open your heart.

You open your mind.

Both will be crushed because you make a miscalculation.

You are not aware of the way The Church has a grasp

on others. You are not aware that people can see someone, open and vulnerable, and think that this is an invitation for them to dump themselves into the chasm of your spirit. You are not aware of how this will inspire these people to try to change who you are, to reform your body and your mind so that you are *their* version of the truth.

You will learn Spanish.

(But at what cost?)

You will feel a deeper connection to a people you have been deprived of knowing.

(But *are* they your people?)

You will still hear the same three words.

Eres un pocho.

Are you?

Did you sell out? Did you give it up?

Are you a rotting fruit? Have the parts of you that give life sloughed away?

Or were these things stolen from you?

(Does it even matter?)

Yes.

It *always* matters.

Eres un pocho.
Eres un pecador.
Eres un joto.
The very community that claimed to love you
to support you
to be your family
will turn its back on you.
A common tongue won't matter

neither will your brown skin

neither will your pleading voice as you beg your godfa-
ther's dad not to do it.

You will be cast out yet again, but this time

this time

you are closer than you ever have been to freedom

because just a couple months later, you will admit to
yourself that you never really believed in God; you were
just *told* to, and you did so because you were afraid.

As that fear floats away, you will press your lips to the
face of a boy

(whose name, in the greatest joke of all time, is Christian)

and it will feel like coming home

(even though you still don't have a home)

because you will realize that all these people held you
back. They twisted your body to fit in their lives. You will
stretch out, elongate your limbs, and you will wrap them
around yourself, around him, and you will feel whole

for the very first time.

You are nineteen.

You have escaped.

You will make your way to Long Beach, to a school
you agreed to go to because it was far, it was paid for, and
because you've heard the stories. You can be yourself in
Long Beach. It has one of the largest gay pride celebra-
tions in the entire world.

There will be happiness. There will be freedom. You
will remember it with fondness when you are older.

But.

You hurt. You don't fit in anywhere. You begin to see how people have rejected you for these differences—you can't help who you love, you can't help that you were adopted, you can't help that you were raised with nothing, you can't help—

You will lash out and hurt others, thinking it is liberation—thinking it is self-determination.

But you *can* help. To say otherwise is to deny culpability, to deny your own agency, to deny that for the first time in your life, you have choices.

Eres un pocho.

Maybe. Because you will begin to understand where that word comes from. You take class after class, and you are given

words

tools

terms

meanings

histories

that you were denied your entire life. As you learn more about what it means to be Latino, what it means to be queer (a name you will soon apply to yourself), you will hear "pocho" in a new light. You will understand that maybe some people *were* mean to you, but there is a deep well of trauma behind it.

That word.

It comes from a people who have been stepped on.

Pressed down.

Who have been told

they can't be smart

they can't be whole
they can't be unique
they can't be themselves
who came to a place that asked them to rot themselves
to twist themselves into violent shapes
to be anything other than what they actually are.
And they? They refused to do it.
And you? You were a reminder of that.
(Not a cause, of course, though sometimes a contributor.)
You are not rotting.
You did not sell anyone out.
But you *can*.
It is a distinction you must learn.
You *will* learn.

You are twenty.

You are queer. You are brown. You are out and proud and scared and confused and excited and every possible contradiction all at once. But you *get* to be all those things, and as hard as it is sometimes, you have the freedom to be a hot fucking mess.

You are twenty-two.

You will feel like your life is an endless cycle of chaos and instability: you grasp on to something—anything—to make you feel more alive. But someone will reduce you down to one part of you. In this case . . . it is your skin color. You are targeted for not being white, and you are driven out of a job. It does not matter how wrong this is, how obviously biased your manager will be throughout the process, or how badly constructed the lies are that cost you your means of survival.

It is a terrible way to learn a lesson that every so often, another Latino will be the worst person in the world.

You imagined solidarity where there was none.

You imagined camaraderie where there was ambition and pride.

You imagined certainty, but the only thing certain about your life, at twenty-two, is chaos.

You will lose a job
a paycheck
an education
a home
everything
but guess what?
You survive it.

You are twenty-four.

You have made it to Los Angeles, twenty-four years after you were born there.

In many ways, the city has welcomed you back. You crawl toward certainty and stability, and soon, you will have your first apartment, all to yourself. It is a small studio in MacArthur Park, located next door to your work, and in a neighborhood that feels like it could be home. Mama's Tamales is a two-minute walk away. You practice your Spanish every day in the swap meets and grocery stores and the panaderia that sells vegan sweets. You start cycling around the city, and you begin to find yourself part of a community: most of them brown and

Black, most of them poor or scraping by like you, many of them queer, and all of them willing to accept you as you are.

You fall in love. He is Latino like you. You will be together for years. And even when it falls apart, it still feels like a success. (Much later, of course.) Because until it happened, and until it ended, you didn't know it was possible to be loved like that.

You are twenty-five.

You once believed that if you were a good person and did what was necessary, you would be spared.

You will learn the hard way—

again and again and again

—that this system cares not for these things. To them you will always be

a failure

a criminal

a cheat

a thug

un ladrón.

No one calls you that other thing anymore. You haven't heard "pocho" in years.

But now you know that there are so many more worse things to be called.

Eres un mojado.

Or

as the officer says to you

as he swings his baton down

fucking wetback

he will never be held accountable for this.

Not just the word

not just the violence

not just the things that he will put in your head, that will haunt you for the rest of your life.

No.

He will never be held accountable for the fact that he mixed you up with another brown person

and that was the reason he tried to end your life.

But he didn't end your life.

Nothing did.

You often heard when you were younger that people like you didn't make it.

You didn't get into school

or win awards

or create art

and you certainly didn't make it to adulthood.

But . . .

You are thirty.

You are in Oakland.

You are so fully yourself. More than you ever have been. Love comes again, love leaves again. But you are inching ever closer to your wildest dreams coming true.

Please.

Hold on.

Just a little bit longer.

It will be worth it.

All those words you wrote as a kid—that you wrote in high school, desperate for someone to hear you, to *see* you—they are paying off in ways you will never begin to imagine.

You will get an idea. It comes from a moment of terrible pain, but you transform that pain into something else.

A story.

You are thirty-six.

You will love your skin, the way it turns a deep, golden brown in the sun.

You will love your journey with the language that once haunted you, and you will come to a place where you can write it. Where you can question it. Where you can see it not as a flaw in your character but as another wonderful part of the world.

You will be yourself.

(Finally.)

And you *are* the writer you have always been. It's just that other people finally see it.

Did you know?

Did you know that just like that time when you were fourteen

when Ms. Alford handed you *The House on Mango Street*

someone is going to hand a book *you* wrote to a young Latino boy, one who has never read a book from cover to cover in his entire life.

He will approach you at an event, and his friends will be clowning on him as he tries to speak, and he will tell you that your book is the first he ever read,

and then,

he will say,

"I didn't know we got to write."

And when the tears fill your eyes, you will know exactly what he means, because you didn't know either.

But now, you do.

Let that breath out.

Breathe it back in.

Are you ready?

It's time to keep doing the work.

Because you must understand that this dismantling, this analysis, this commitment to action, never ends. It shouldn't. Until this whole rotten system is eradicated, until all bodies are liberated, you will have more to do.

Eres un pocho.

Maybe. But you can be so much more.

The Price of Admission

Naima Coster

I didn't meet my father-in-law until eight years after I started dating the man who would become my husband. By then, he'd missed so much of our life—graduations, our wedding, our move from New York City to North Carolina. He was sent to prison when we were newly dating undergrads at Yale. Years later, he was deported back to Colombia. Although I'd never met him, he was both known and unknown to me—a notorious protagonist of several difficult, heartbreaking family stories. And yet, he was also absent, the subject of great silence. My in-laws told tales of the damage he'd done, but they also seemed not to want to talk about him.

I was no stranger to family silences, secrets, or shame. As a girl, I'd heard *A la gente le gusta hablar* often, a warning that anything I told someone could be repeated and used as a weapon against me down the line. I heard, too, *Don't go telling people all your private business*. And, perhaps, my least favorite: *You represent us* as a reminder that I was a symbol of my family. The way I behaved and looked, the things I said and told weren't really about me—they were about the people I came from and showing others that we were good, deserving of respect.

We decided to fly to Bogotá for a scant three days during a short vacation my husband took off from his medical residency. Every child with living parents is one day haunted by the question, *How much time do we have left*? The question felt especially urgent for us. My father-in-law, whom I'll call Angel here, has schizophrenia and struggles with addiction. In Colombia, without support or family, he has been, at times, without a home. As a doctor, my husband knew the statistics about life expectancy and untreated schizophrenia, addiction, and homelessness. We couldn't dawdle.

Before we left, my in-laws advised me to be careful with Angel. I shouldn't trust him, or he'd take advantage—I had to stay alert because he lived in a dangerous part of the city. They worried my husband would be vulnerable because of his sympathy and feelings for his father—I had to be the levelheaded one. Their warnings made me anxious, but mostly I was curious. I wanted to meet the man my husband came from, the one who'd loved him and lived with him, who'd hurt him and left, and then, eventually, was taken away. He was a part of the story of the person I loved most, and he'd become a part of my story, too. I wanted one day to have a child, and Angel would be a part of her legacy: her blood, her origin story.

I am no stranger to a complicated family history. Growing up, I often felt that the life my mother and her siblings had led in the Dominican Republic was the stuff of legend, more dramatic and intense than anything in the novels I devoured. Their stories were of adultery and jail time, betrayal and knife fights, hunger and poverty, splintered marriages, divided families, alcoholism, depression, and grief. In one story, one relative was thrown off a roof. There was so much violence, so many injuries and losses. The stories ended with the family arriving in the United States.

I realize now that elevating those family hardships into myths was one of the ways we coped. In these epic versions of the past, there were heroes and villains, plot twists, and devastating irony. It all seemed to hurt a little less if it was a capital-S story instead of the hard facts of their lives.

My father's family was from Cuba and Curaçao, and there were fewer stories about this side—more silence in response to my questions. Now I see this as a different strategy for dealing with a difficult past: doing what you could to bury the facts, to keep quiet, so that the stories and the pain don't get passed on.

It isn't lost on me that in becoming a writer I've tried to forge my own, different approach to family history. I try neither to sensationalize nor to cover up. I write to understand, to live inside experiences that interest me or excite me or haunt me. I write as a way to move away from shame.

Shame was one of my most constant companions as a girl—it is with me still. I took to heart the mission of being a respectable reflection of my parents and family because I could see why they worried so much about how they were seen. They'd been turned away from opportunities, targeted by police, ridiculed by neighbors' gossip, and criticized for things they couldn't always control or hide. In one of my mother's stories of her girlhood, she was turned away from a cousin's birthday party because her clothes weren't nice enough—she and her brothers looked so visibly poor after their father was sent to jail. I believed myself a potential endnote to the family story, the apotheosis. I could be the one who lived the American dream, who made money and moved to a coveted neighborhood. I could earn out on the gamble the family had made when they came to this country. I could be the reason they'd endured so much pain.

When I got a scholarship to a selective, private school, the pressure I felt intensified. I wasn't rich like my classmates; I wasn't white. I was Black, Latina, a Brooklyn girl, a daughter and granddaughter of immigrants. I was an outsider, but I had the opportunity to become an *insider* maybe, if I could prove myself and succeed. When I thought of being "good," this was exactly what I envisioned: fitting in, achieving, gaining the approval of people in power, who, at the time, were my parents, my teachers, the white girls in my class. I became obsessed with appearances. I wanted to be eloquent, neat, and competent. I wanted to earn As, to get my curly hair to stay down and stay in place. I tried to avoid mistakes, any signs of weakness. I saw this as the price of admission, and I wanted to belong.

It took me years to see that what I thought of as goal-oriented was tainted, defined by the logic of white supremacy—the idea that there was something wrong with me, that I wasn't deserving of opportunity or dignity just as I was. Inside me, there was a voice that said, *Because of who you are and your history, you will never be enough.*

We met Angel downtown, in el Centro, a busy commercial area ringed by green mountains. I was stunned by how much he reminded me of my husband: it wasn't just their appearance, although they shared several features: a creased, broad brow, pouting lips, feathery lashes. It was the habits they shared that shocked me, the ways they seemed to mimic each other, although they'd been separated by distance and years. Angel swung his arms when he walked. He sang to himself during lulls in our conversation. He arched his eyebrows to begin a story.

I couldn't help thinking my husband would look like Angel someday, although not completely. I expected he'd look less battered and squeezed by life. Angel was leaner than in the photographs I'd seen—he was missing teeth, there were gaps in his smile. His clothes were simple, inexpensive—although I got the impression he'd dressed up for us. He was chatty and warm, delighted to see his son. He got my name wrong, but I didn't hold it against him. He led the way, showing us around the city that was now his home. I knew how special time like this could be: moments of togetherness and calm after so much hardship and loss. The day was pleasant, anticlimactic.

The next day, our second of three in Bogotá, we called Angel and couldn't reach him. We went down to el Centro anyway, and he never showed. We decided to make the best of it and explore the city on foot. We had a tinto somewhere—coffee dusted with cinnamon, sweetened with panela. I was full of rage that he'd ghosted on us when we had so few days to spend with him after we'd flown across an ocean, and after all the years he'd already been missing. But I held my tongue, unsure whether we'd see him at all on our last day in Colombia.

We did. I don't remember if he explained why we couldn't reach him the day before. Either way, we didn't make much of it. I followed my husband's lead, and we carried on. We decided to go to a museum, and they posed for pictures together in the gallery. Angel wore a blue and white striped shirt, and he stood a foot shorter than my husband. In the pictures, he looks prim and small with my husband's arm thrown around him. It's as if their roles are reversed: my husband is the proud father, Angel the child who longs to be gathered close.

The rest of the day is a blur. We must have eaten—there are more pictures at a café. We might have had buñuelos or pan de bono. What I know for certain is that at the café, Angel recited poems. He read aloud from a collection I bought on the day he didn't show. After, we rode the bus until it was time for us to part ways. As the bus pulled up to Angel's stop, he asked us for money. My husband pulled out his wallet, rifled through, then handed him the pesos. They embraced and said goodbye. This was in the spring of 2016. We haven't seen him since.

When we first learned Angel would be deported, what we most feared was the prospect of going years without seeing him. Back then, while he was still serving his sentence, we did what we could try to keep him in the country, but we had limited options, time, and money. My husband was in medical school, and I was earning a degree in writing. Still, we consulted with advocates to see if we could keep him—a permanent legal resident—in the US after he served his time. They were frank. It didn't matter that he lived with a serious disability and would be without familial support in Colombia; his parents, siblings, and children were all in the US. It didn't matter that we'd miss out on a future with him if he was sent away. He wasn't a Dreamer, or an asylum seeker, or a blameless child. His case wouldn't garner much empathy or leniency. He wasn't a good immigrant.

I understand the appeal of the idea of the "good immigrant." I've heard it used by immigration advocates, Latinx people, and my own family as they've worked to build a case for why we should be welcomed in the US, not only legally and officially, but also culturally, in a nation's narrative and account of itself. The impulse to prove our virtue has become all the more intense during the era of Trump, who has made a point of demonizing people of color and immigrants.

Immigrants are hard workers, we say. Immigrants work the essential jobs that keep America running. Immigrants are mothers and fathers, innocent children, good people who do not deserve to be separated from their families, put in cages, tear-gassed, or lost. In building these arguments, we lay bare how terrifyingly distorted our sense of justice is—our sense of mercy. No one should be put in a cage. Families shouldn't be separated. These rights are fundamental and aren't contingent on someone's presumed virtue.

And the idea that we can earn our dignity is deceptive. When has virtue ever been sufficient to save Black and brown lives? Who gets to decide what virtue is or who is virtuous? And aren't we all much more multidimensional and messy than "bad" or "good"? Or is that complexity reserved only for white people—US citizens?

I often think about what we lose when we deny the complexity of our stories, our families, and ourselves in service of some victorious narrative—the desire to declare ourselves triumphant, worthy, palatable to whiteness. I think about the testimonies and self-expression we lose, as well as the opportunities to accept ourselves and connect to one another.

During my years in private school, I slipped into a deep depression. The pressure to be good, to prove myself, was a vise that was ever-tightening. In my life at home, I was also lonely and hurting. My parents were unwell, and they harmed me, as they harmed each other and themselves. I did what I could to hide my misery, and I was convinced I was doing a good job. I still participated in class; I earned good grades; I was chipper and compliant, and sharp when I needed to be. And yet, there were days I hid under the cover of my black hoodie, pulled over my uniform, and I scrawled sad lyrics on the inside of my forearms in pen and slumped in corners with my headphones on, listening to devastating songs. The people who cared about me were paying attention—my teachers, my friends. One girl, whom I'll call M here, told her mother I was depressed, and her mother approached my parents after a school recital. She told them she was worried I'd hurt myself. She said she thought I needed help.

I didn't overhear the conversation, and so I don't know what my parents said in return. I only know what they said to me. They told me to be careful with M and not to talk to her anymore. They reminded me of the risks of going around telling people my business. They didn't ask if I was depressed. They didn't ask if I needed help.

This was not the last time something like this happened. Other friends, other adults, sought to help me, but no one got through. My family closed the door on any outside intervention, and I, too, felt that I had to cover up my problems, anything that reflected poorly on me, on us. I stopped being friends with M, although I never explained why. We used to talk about *Buffy* on our long train rides home. We used to dance in the halls and crack jokes and curl our bodies around each other and nuzzle together during after-school meetings. But I started to see her only as someone who'd exposed me, who'd nearly ruined the performance I believed was the only way I could survive.

By the time I learned I was pregnant in my thirties, I'd spent more than a decade trying to unlearn my obsession with being good. I'd staged several rebellions, some small—cutting off all my hair, getting a tattoo. Other rebellions were tremendous—declining to go to medical school like my parents wanted me to, moving out of my childhood apartment at twenty-three so I could have more freedom, living with my boyfriend before we were married. I began trying to tell the truth about my inner life and family, even the unseemly parts, in the way that I knew how: through writing.

And yet, being pregnant triggered an old perfectionism in me. I wanted to be a *good* pregnant person just as I wanted to be a *good* mother. I even felt the urge to be a good patient, as if my doctor's visits were tests I could score an *A* on if I gained the "right" amount of weight and did prenatal yoga and took my vitamins and managed my stress. I was smug when people noticed that my ankles weren't swollen or that I had plenty of energy for someone in the third trimester. I took credit for these things as if they reflected only how well I could follow the rules. I did little to acknowledge the role of luck and privilege—the randomness of my genes. I still wasn't over needing the affirmation that I was doing things right.

When my due date came and went, and my doctor scheduled a labor induction, all my smugness dissolved. I was finally confronting what so many pregnant people face at one point or another: a lack of control over my own body and experience. I knew I couldn't make myself go into labor spontaneously, but I tried anyway. I ate fistfuls of dates; I drank herbal tea; I walked for miles and miles in the humid, mid-Atlantic heat. I did all the things I'd been told to do, and still, nothing worked. I sobbed and sobbed and blamed myself. This was the underside of my arrogance, my self-satisfaction—if things went wrong, I could just as quickly turn and decide I was no good.

The induction wasn't wanted, and I was devastated. Still, my daughter came, leading my husband and me into an entirely new life. This is what has surprised me about motherhood—how near mourning is to joy. As I've watched my daughter grow, I have celebrated her and adored her, and I have also grieved. I've grieved the things I've lacked as a daughter, as well as the things I won't be able to give her.

She is still too young to ask about Angel, but she won't be for long. I don't know whether she'll ever meet him in person, but I don't believe they will be close. It is a loss for her, for him, our whole family.

I wonder what stories we'll tell her and how we'll explain who Angel is, what he's been through, and what it has meant for all of us. Other people are missing in her life, other relatives whose reputations precede them. How will we explain their absence? How will we describe who they are and how they came to no longer be in our lives, her life? Will we manage to avoid the tropes of heroes and villains when we tell her about the people she comes from, the ones she knows and the ones she never will? I hope so. What I'm certain we will say to her is this: You don't have to be perfect to deserve a good life. You don't have to be good to be missed.

Caution Song

Natasha Diaz

When digging around someone's insides
it is common practice, at minimum,
to use a local anesthetic. Consider that
the next time you cut me open,
just after we are introduced on a roof,
where unlike the melted rubber
on top of my building, there is a finished floor.

Ribs spread so wide, you can see through
to the sun as it lowers its head, waking
the city to the magenta sky and
my nerve endings. As you search
for this part of me that is so unlike you,
know that I can't open my mouth
because the scream is hard and loud—
but this party just started,
and a scene would
kill the mood.

Elbow deep in my curves
I ease you out of me

but we both know sewing me back together is not your
  job—
So I listen to your straight lines
and pinch my skin
to keep any more of me from getting lost in your history.

If I could speak, I would say
that I come from fallen stars
who crashed into the ocean, arriving—
on the sand of Praia do Porto da Barra as women
you have been taking from—for years.

And that I will try to find myself
between the person I thought I was
and who you expected—
Not find exactly, but
Readjust, not readjust, exactly, but
Agitate, not agitate, exactly, but
Dissect, not dissect, exactly, but
Detract, not detract, exactly, but
Compartmentalize, not compartmentalize, exactly,
But unable to just be—for years.

I would tell you
that wrapping myself up
as your party favor
is not a gift
But no one told me
I could be my own.

You tell me it can't be true
that my great-grandmother escaped the pogroms in
    Ukraine
at the same time that my great-grandmother—
a descendant of the enslaved—
returned to Africa.
There is no proof, you say,
that my great-grandmother stood,
feet in the soil of Itarana, Bahia
and planted the seeds that would become me
But then turn up the music—
and tell me to dance—
so maybe, you might see my Vovo in my hips.

I've heard it before,
that you probably mean no harm
when you challenge me to speak
    in a language
I only know in lullabies and your curiosity
Is an opportunity for growth I should nurture—
I would say that I have no interest
    in gardening
But this party has gone on long enough now
for me to open my mouth to sing
with the sirens, then wipe the blood from my lips
as you run down the stairs.

Had you heeded my caution song,
you would have known

that I filed my teeth before I left the house,
and saved yourself a swollen mouth.

Because if you call me spicy,
you should expect me to bite your tongue.

The Mark of a Good Man

Meg Medina

My mother was already diagnosed with late-stage colon cancer when we found ourselves at her bank in Sunrise, Florida, a few years ago. I was helping her close her accounts. In a few weeks, she'd be packing up her Corningware and coming to live with me in Virginia, and we were both feeling unsure about what was ahead.

We went to Chase Manhattan, a few blocks from her condo where she'd retired twenty years before. She wanted to transfer her account to a branch in my state, but we were informed that there were none. We would have to close the account, the clerk told us, and start a new one elsewhere when she resettled.

Ma sat with her black leather purse in her lap, more agitated than when Dr. Gupta explained her tumors. She asked the clerk again and again if he was sure there were no Chase branches near me.

¿Como puede ser? How could that be, she wanted to know, an important bank like this? She'd had an account at Chase for fifty years, she told him a little too loudly in that cubicle—more years than the clerk had been alive!— all the way back to her early days in New York.

What she didn't tell him:

Chase had been the only bank to approve the loans she needed to bring her parents and siblings here—including Francisco, her baby brother.

A few months after she died, I found myself remembering that day. I'd been going through my mother's papers, the important ones—divorce papers, rent receipts—that she kept in a hard-shell blue suitcase securely fastened with an old macramé belt in her closet. Two things caught my eye. First was my mother's plane ticket receipt from Cuba, tucked in an old Pan American Airlines folio. She'd flown from Havana to the US on May 10, 1960, and paid $223.47 for the flight, a small fortune sixty years ago.

I stared at that carbon copy of the ticket, thinking of how hard it has always been for refugees and for Ma in particular. Three years after she arrived, my father stepped out of her life with a new woman on his arm and right into the American dream as a surgeon. Ma was left wearing a full set of dentures at forty-two, working a factory job in Queens, and raising two difficult girls on her own.

The second thing I pulled from the suitcase was a letter my father wrote back to my tía Gregoria, not long after my mother brought her to the US. The oldest of the siblings, Gregoria, took a hard look at my mother's budget and at the sofa bed Ma shared with me. She found my father's office address on one of his $150.00 alimony checks and wrote to ask him to send us more money.

His reply, written in the fancy penmanship that you don't see anymore: No, he would not send more child support. He was facing many expenses himself. However,

Ma could send the girls to him during any vacation, he said. We would always be welcome in his home, an offer it would turn out he'd regret making. Or else, he added, my mother should find herself an Americano like she always said she might do.

I don't know if Ma secretly wanted an American man to save her. If so, she kept it to herself, never dating a single person throughout my life. In fact, of all the advice she force-fed me, being wary of men was her favorite, even though she had a father and a brother she loved back in Cuba. *Ya sabes como son*, she often warned me. *Te engañan*. And what was worse than being played for a fool?

I don't know why the officers at Chase loaned her the money to fly her parents and siblings here to the States, either. She was hardly a safe bet to pay it back. Did her pale skin help? Her old teaching degree? Anti-communism when we were all still practicing our bomb shelter drills? Or, did she mention, as she sometimes did to suggest her daughters' worth, that our father was a doctor, carving out with surgical care the bit about his being a player?

Did those things make her a safe bet?

Anyway, I've kept both documents, just as she did, each a piece of the rompecabezas of how good men, bad men, and migration shaped my mother's life—and mine.

I met my father for the first time when I was about four, I think. He had come to the apartment with Abuelo Nestor to visit Carmela and me. By then, he was married and having kids with Linda, the blonde nurse from Pennsylvania he'd met while he was still married to Ma. His scandalous exit a few weeks before my birth and his total absence thereafter became a permanent stain—an affliction. Without a father who lived with us, my neighbors and, soon enough, my teachers at school said I came from a broken home.

The day of the visit, my father brought me a plush bunny with a wind-up silver crank on its yellow bottom that played "Rock-a-Bye Baby." There were wires in the rabbit's satin-lined ears to keep them straight. I played on the floor as Ma served café negro in demitasses, silent—the last defense of a wronged wife. Then, somehow, the wires inside the rabbit's ears snapped.

It would be another decade before I laid eyes on my father again.

There were no phone calls or letters between us during that time—no birthday wishes or presents or surprises during the holidays. I didn't miss him at all. He simply wasn't a reality. In fact, there isn't a single photograph of my father and me at all, not from then or at any other time after. It is as if we didn't exist in each other's lives.

Years later, the woman who would become my mother-in-law made me wonder about that unnatural detachment. She was a family friend of sorts, working in the same transistor factory that left the scent of cleaning solvents clinging to my mother's clothes.

"Men only love their children through their wives," she told me one day. "That's why we have to be smart."

It was a statement she'd repeat again in our many conversations together over the years. I heard it over a Monte Cristo sandwich at A&S's restaurant, in her apartment in

Queens, at my kitchen table in Florida, while my husband changed our son's diaper on the bed in the next room.

Each time, I hated the stink of blame in that idea. How was it a woman's job to keep a man from wandering or to bind him to his own children? I thought of the boys I had known in high school, eager to slide their hands inside a girl's jeans and pronounce her a whore. Was that our fault, too?

Still, I never could deny that my father's attachments to us had been easily unraveled, not the kind of primal tie that makes a mother's breast milk leak at the sound of her baby's cry.

Had Ma not been smart somehow? I hated myself for wondering.

Meeting my mother's gente was no smoother the next year. Ma announced that they were coming from Cuba at last, away from Fidel. I was thrilled, mostly because I could, at long last, be free of my babysitter, Nené, a Cuban lady with red hair and pudgy fingers who forced me to take naps. My real abuela would now be my babysitter, I told Nené when I fired her all on my own.

I remember the cab pulling up in front of our building on 158th Street. Abuelo and Abuela, Tía Gregoria and Tía Rosa, all of them got out in shabby, refugee center coats. I watched from the window as the driver pulled their suitcases from the trunk and then listened to their steps echo as they climbed toward me. That first night, they slept in the cheap rollaway beds in our living room.

It didn't take long to find out these relatives would need

help in a way that seemed strange to me since they were adults. My aunts didn't know very much about even obvious things, I soon realized, like how the intercom worked in the lobby or which apartment number was ours. All the units, they claimed, looked the same. Ma tried to teach them a million details, but sometimes the learning didn't stick. When Tía Rosa knocked on Mr. Miller's door after we'd walked back from the A&P, her lip twitching with nerves, I was mortified. His blue eyes slid over me, and I knew what he was thinking. Was I dumb enough to forget where I lived? It was right upstairs, directly above his place. But what could I do? Tía Rosa was the adult, and she had insisted that his apartment was ours, even when I argued the obvious.

I don't know when I became aware that I had an uncle, too. My tío Francisco wasn't there yet. He'd come in later, full of self-assurance and daring, in so many ways my aunts' opposite.

Maybe his name was tucked in the conversations that swirled around me in the kitchen where I liked to play with the plastic fruit. Or maybe he was mentioned when my aunts read aloud the letters sent to us by airmail on onionskin paper from the island. In whatever way it happened, a marvelous genie took shape before I ever met him.

My tío Francisco was tall and guapo, my aunts said. Women loved him. He had slick hair, even better than Desi Arnaz, and he was a whiz with numbers, too. He couldn't wait to meet me. He was still in Cuba, though, pasando hambre y trabajo along with his wife and daughter. Our family's plan? Pool money together again fast—find a way to shimmy them out.

But what I most remember from that haze is a piece of information that seemed impossible no matter how I puzzled over it. It was the thing my family only whispered because it was so bad.

Tío Francisco had been in prison.

Francisco and his wife, Elba, were trying to help her nephew.

Tía Rosa tells me this as she is resting in her bed at Canterbury rehabilitation facility last week. Even when she's in a fresh diaper, this room reeks of piss. I'm holding the spoon out to her, trying to coax her to eat one more bite.

I stop as soon as she says it.

"Hiding him from what, Tía?" I ask. We've been talking about my uncle, specifically about his time in jail.

Rosa closes her eyes. "I don't remember. The army, maybe?" My aunt is eighty-six now, and some days she doesn't remember that I've been here. Other days, Cuba of long ago is as clear to her as the waters of Varadero.

I pick at the label on the vanilla pudding balanced in my lap. This is new information, something that deviates from the carefully scripted version I was told as a child. How does a good man end up in jail? Francisco had a friend with a boat who offered to take him to Florida. They'd planned to launch their chalana in secret one night from La Isabela, an illegal journey but faster than waiting for the endless paperwork authorizing a legal exit. Unfortunately, a keen-eyed neighbor alerted authorities as part of his civic duty. Tío was sentenced to a year in jail somewhere in Las Villas.

But now there is this—Elba's nephew.

I cobble Tía's words with the shards I've discovered over a lifetime of excavation. *Could* it be that Francisco tried to sneak out of the country to help his wife's nephew? This was the time of El Che and rousing speeches and firing squads and ¡viva la revolución! If Tía Rosa is right, Francisco became a worm and an enemy of the people's revolution by trying to spare someone else some trouble.

"Julito came to tell us that night," Tía Rosa says.

"Julito?" I ask. "Was he a neighbor?" She mumbles an explanation, but it's a mix of names and relationships I don't recognize.

"Did you go visit him while he was in prison?" I probe.

Quiet. For a second, I think she's asleep, but then she shakes her head.

This is not at all what I expect. He was her only brother, three years her senior. Why abandon him that way?

There may be other reasons for her lack of visits that she won't tell. A disagreement with his wife? Blame, maybe? I don't know. Frail as she is, my aunt is stubborn, and the women in this family were always prone to disagreements.

Tía shuts her eyes. "Just your grandmother went from our house. To take him food."

I think back to Abuela Bena, the hives that sprang upon her skin when she first arrived in Queens. The smell of vinegar on the paper towels she pressed against her slippered feet to quiet the itch that was diagnosed as nerves. I try to picture a younger version of her visiting her son in jail, and suddenly I think of my own son, living fancy in New York with his girlfriend. Would I try to rip open bars to free him from jail, strangle guards, scratch my skin to blood?

"It must have been hard for her," I tell Rosa. "Her son . . ."

"Figúrate," Tía Rosa whispers, and then she motions my spoon away. She's had enough.

By the time I was eight, the men were gone, extinguished in el exilio one way or another. My father was living with his wife and six new kids. They had a rambling house in the woods of Massachusetts.

Both my grandfathers were dead, too: Nestor, to the sudden slam of a heart attack as he walked by a television repair shop and Clemento, Ma's father, a few months later, to a cancer that left him groaning in the bedroom the year I was in second grade. I had to whisper at home every day so as not to disturb him while he died.

After, there were explanations for our manless predicament, shared while sweating over the stove, hauling groceries, or figuring out how to do simple apartment repairs with dime-store tools. If only we had our men, life would be easier, they complained. But in the next breath, they pivoted. What could you do against God when it came to dead men? You had to console yourself with whatever He sent your way. El Señor knew what he was doing.

As for the runners, like my father, ese descarado, there was nothing to be done about that either. His heartlessness had been hiding. It had been an ugly seed watered into bloom by his illusions of the good American life.

But then, when Tío Francisco finally arrived in the US, it was as if there was hope of changing all that.

Ma and her sisters were electric with anticipation that swept me up, too. No one from Cuba could travel directly to the US anymore. You had to petition a third country to take you in first. Francisco and Elba had chosen Spain. Tío Francisco would come to the US first and then arrange for her travel to join him after that.

When he stepped out of the yellow cab, he was holding an enormous Spanish doll, one that stood almost to my waist. She had caramel skin, green eyes, and darker hair than my old doll, Velvet, whose blonde hair grew out of a hole in her head if you pulled it. Tío's doll wore a red cap and a matching skirt. I was almost nine, budding breasts and practically leaving dolls behind entirely, but I instantly loved her.

And him.

There is a picture I keep of me with Francisco that day. He looks every bit the stereotype of a handsome Cuban man, just as my aunts had promised. His hair is slicked back, and he wears wire-rimmed 1970s aviators. We are at Ma's Formica dining room table, all smiles. Francisco is here in the flesh, at last, and all of us women and girls are rejoicing. We are not alone and vulnerable in this country, the way Abuela hates. Something about his presence is a cloak of protection. He makes things right again.

My sister, in a paisley jumper and long hair, is half cut off in the frame, compliments most likely of Ma's crap photography. (There are old albums filled with headless people to prove it.) But I am whole. I wear a grey dress, biting my lip, my hair in a ponytail. I'm standing on a chair beside him, and so I look almost as tall as my new uncle. The doll is between us.

In that picture, you can see the blinding crush of happiness. Somehow, I already know that my home is a little less broken.

I claimed him after that, completely and without reservation.

I made him Father's Day cards at school and drew pictures of us holding hands.

I slipped my bare feet inside his big clown shoes and clomped around Abuela's apartment until he laughed.

I wrote an essay saying I'd gone to Spain to visit him, although I never had, and the lie, when discovered, embarrassed Ma in front of my teacher.

I pored over the picture he showed me of his wife, Elba, on a wrought-iron balcony back in Spain, where she was waiting for her papers. I marveled at how pretty she was, wondering if maybe I could go live with them, especially while their daughter still waited for permission to leave Cuba and join them.

When I slept over on Tía Gregoria's sofa bed in the living room, I would spring up early in the morning and find his long body splayed on one of those old rollaway beds that my aunts had jammed against a wall for him in the kitchen. I waited at the edge of his thin mattress until he lit up a Winston, staring at the ceiling, thinking about God knows what. When the coffeepot gurgled, Abuela would bring him his first cup of black coffee of the day. I watched him sit up to drink and finish his smoke. He'd turn to me at last, smile, tug my hair as a hello, my heart melting.

There are specific places in a home you remember. I have a bathroom in mind, the one in Abuela's house.

There was a time, before Francisco was with us, when Tía Gregoria and Tía Rosa insisted I should not be bathed in the same tub as the adults. It was, they said, unsanitary. Children should be properly bathed in stand-alone tubs perched on little wheels like they'd done back home. Little girls should be sprinkled with agua de violetas afterward.

They wanted to spare me the filth of adults, I suppose. They wanted—maybe needed—a way of raising me that they understood from home.

I don't know where they found the refrigerator drawer that became my tub. Maybe on a large trash day. But someone got the idea—probably Tía Rosa—that it was the perfect size for skinny me, a little scrawny for my age. And so began the habit of putting the drawer inside the bathtub at Abuela's and bathing me there. The hard, plastic ripples along the bottom of the thing made marks on my skin that lasted long after I'd been dried off and rubbed down with Jean Naté, the substitute for violet water.

That's what I remember most about that bathroom. Except for Tío.

My aunts' closet was near the bathroom, too. I liked to stand inside it and watch him shaving in the mirror—hair on faces was new. One morning, he stopped his razor, a streak of foam missing along his cheek. He turned to face me, aware I'd been there all along.

"Niña, tell me this. Do men shave their armpits here?"

I didn't know what to say as he stood there, handsome in his sleeveless undershirt. He was asking me something important, but what was the right answer? I wasn't aware of people's armpits, and I had no access to hombres except him. My mother refused to date, after all, and there were never male visitors besides two distant cousins, Wilson and Mongo, who were always in trouble, so Ma never liked to have them around.

He must have seen my blank stare. "Never mind," he said, laughing, as he turned back to his whiskers.

And then there is another tiny bathroom memory, so small I wonder if I have imagined it. Francisco opening the bathroom door and calling Tía Gregoria, the sensible sister, inside. They whispered as I watched from my closet, hiding among the polyester blouses and Woolworth handkerchiefs.

Years later, Tía Gregoria told me how they first thought Tío might be as sick as he was.

"It was the sound of air when he peed," she told me. "Like a balloon. And then those drops of blood on the rim."

People say uncles fill a key piece in a kid's life, especially when a father is missing. You read that all the time. It was true for me.

But it's also true that nieces can fill spaces, too. Maybe I already knew I had that tiny power to make him feel important here. Maybe, in that way, we made each other less lonely.

Anyway, it was Tío Francisco who taught me things my mother and aunts didn't, like how to read en español. They'd meant to do it, but with work and my mother's long depressive naps and all the rest, no one had actually done it. One day, he wrote out the vowels on loose-leaf paper while we were sitting in Abuela's living room. He told me their sounds and made me repeat them: *ah, eh, ee, o, ooh.* He promised that those sounds never changed, no matter what. Spanish wasn't fickle in its rules about letters and sounds. Soon enough, I was reading a passage aloud for him easily. My aunts pronounced me brilliant. But their eyes were even shinier for their brother, who'd taught me, sweetly, lovingly, as if I were his own child.

Even now, whenever I read anything in Spanish—my own books included—my mind crawls back up on that couch where we sat together side by side.

It was Tío Francisco, too, who showed me how to have nerve. He landed a job in the bookkeeping department at the Hilton Hotel on Sixth Avenue and Fifty-Third Street in Manhattan; all his whiz-bang math skills trumped his stumbling English. It was an hour away from where we lived, an unheard-of distance from Abuela's horrifying view. He rode the subway and changed at the right stop, unafraid of being mugged the way Abuela warned would happen to Ma and my aunts if they dared work anywhere but the transistor factory close to home. He smelled of drugstore aftershave and wore a suit and tie, not a jumper with his name on a patch. Watching him return each day safely, I learned that it was possible to go farther than anyone expected.

I wonder if he thought that all good things were possible now that he was living his own American dream? Maybe so—and he was letting me be part of it. One day he talked his boss into selling him an old upright piano, a leftover from the hotel's recent renovation. I was thrilled as the delivery men hauled it up the steps and around the bend for all my neighbors to see. He wanted me to learn to play, he explained, the way his little girl had done back in Cuba, the metronome marking the beat as her pretty fingers danced on the keys.

Was it his hope? Was I just a placeholder for his daughter? I didn't think about those things as a girl. In the meantime, what was the harm in pretending he was all mine?

I don't know how the argument first started. But tempers were high in Abuela's teeny apartment.

I wanted something, but what? A toy? Permission to go somewhere? Attention? Did I not like what they were talking about? No se. That part of the memory is blank.

Tío was home from work, though, and it was unusual. Looking back, it could have been one of the many doctors' appointments revealing the bad news.

Again, the information is blank.

But the tension, *that* is very clear, and how I was getting mouthier, an ugly habit now that I was almost eleven.

It was Tío who finally raised his voice to shut me up.

"Coño, ya!" He snapped at me, cursing and telling me in a stern voice to stop being a malcriada.

By then, he was feeling sick and likely tired of that roll-away bed. Like me, he was straining against my aunts' meddling, not to mention my grandmother's nerves. And privately—because how could he not?—he was surely figuring, with a bookkeeper's exactness, the needs pressing in on him from all around. An apartment of his own, a way to unlock the desperation that was taking hold of his stranded wife in Spain, yet another pile of money to get their daughter out of Cuba after that. A doctor to get him well.

I thought of none of that.

Instead, I stared at him hard, suddenly unsure of everything between us, in that all-or-nothing way of being young. Men fooled you into loving them, didn't they? Well, not me. I took my hardest verbal swing on the one topic I had been asked never to bring up to my uncle.

"You're not my father. I don't have to listen to you," I spat. "You're just an uncle. And you're a bad man, too. That's why they sent you to jail! They should have left you there."

Somebody sucked in a sharp breath, and then the apartment fell silent.

Tío Francisco looked at me in a way that I won't ever forget. I had violated something precious between us, a sacred place of comfort for both of us. He pulled himself to his full six feet and, without a sound, walked out to the kitchen.

Tía Gregoria came to where I was sitting on the couch. I was red-faced and crying now, trying to be the injured one. The damning words I'd used to insult my uncle were still floating over my head.

"Go ask him for forgiveness," she said with deadly calm, and then she left me alone in my misery.

It was never the same between us again.

His wife and daughter came to New York, one soon after the other. Together they moved out of Abuela's place into their own first-floor apartment several blocks away on Sanford Avenue. And even though I made a welcome sign on posterboard for Elba and tried my best to be pleasing to my cousin, I couldn't change the fact that he belonged to them more than he did to me. I was old enough to know it was true.

In the spring of the year I turned thirteen, a rich girl named Patty Hearst got convicted of bank robbery. Our country was making preparations to celebrate the 200th birthday of the Declaration of Independence with Operation Sail, a parade of tall ships in the Hudson, and a fireworks display unlike any other. That year, too, while I faced a bully in school, Ma and my aunts made long and fretful car drives to the hospital where Tío Francisco and, as unbelievable as it was macabre, Elba both lay dying of cancer.

Disease finished its march through Tío Francisco's life with a vengeance that was bigger than all the illusions I had of him and bigger than all the hopes he'd had of a new life here in this country. It took Elba in March and then him a few weeks later, in our own version of a Greek tragedy. Cancer claimed them the way it had taken Abuelo Clemento, the way it would find Tía Gregoria eleven years later and Ma, many years after that. All of us in the family dying, I thought, of unfulfilled longings, deep and secretive, clamped inside our gut with no way out.

Francisco was wearing his aviator glasses in the casket the day of his funeral. The knot in his cheap tie looked too big, and his hair was white and thin. I could barely recognize him. No amount of embalming makeup could reverse the fact that he'd shriveled to one hundred pounds.

I sat in the long row of chairs at the funeral home, staring ahead at the wreaths of carnations and trying to ignore my mother's face, crumpled with an exhausted sadness she had never allowed me to see before. It was the first time I'd even considered the grit that Ma and my tías had to call up just to survive one loss after another.

I thought back to the times I had badgered her with questions about my uncle and his imprisonment.

"¡Sió!" she had warned me time and again. "Don't talk about that story to anybody, oíste?" She'd made her demand in that loud stage whisper she sometimes used with me as if someone were watching her performance as a mother without a proper man. What would information like that say about us? What kind of people would our American neighbors think we were? Who would understand what Francisco had lived, what any of us had?

Of course, I didn't know. I still don't.

I was still unaware of all the things that would never transpire between Tío and me. No holiday gatherings with petty arguments. No life advice I'd ignore about boys who were too old for me or wolfish. No moment when he could promise me that not every man's heart was a stone.

All of that I would have to learn on my own.

But that day, my shame and regret sat right next to me, edging me toward the chasm of a new cold truth revealed to me that first year of my teens.

Good men and bad men came into your life disguised and with no guarantee of staying. You had to steel yourself to survive them both. My father, costumed as a respectable surgeon, had willingly made a wreckage of our lives in his grab for the American dream. Tío Francisco, the prisoner, had come for that same goal but had run out of luck. In the end, though, he'd been the bigger man.

All these years later, now older myself than he ever got, I miss him still.

The names of people in this essay have been changed to protect their privacy.

#Julian4SpiderMan
Julian Randall

....

OK, people, let's do this one last time. Spider-Man has always been Black. This is the story of one Spider-Man in 1998, and in this universe, he's me. I am six years old, posted up in front of the TV before my first Halloween party. The costume is perfect except for the mask, it is made for everyone, but it also isn't. My hair, like my mother's hair and her mother before her, swells in pitch-black waves like I am told the ocean looks some nights in DR. Beneath the mask, my head looks off-kilter, asymmetrical, as if drawn by someone only half interested. I slick my small hands along the top of the mask, feel the pinpoints of hair poking through, and wish they wouldn't. For the first time I can remember, I feel powerful and unmanageable all at once. This is a lesson in the interior, in what is known but never taught. There are masks we are born into and masks we can't hope to fit. I slick my hands over the mask again. I am the stubble insisting through the polyester, new grass in a country of no rain.

But this isn't the story of how the mask is ruined—it's ruined because I can't see shit out of it. There are eyeholes, but they're narrow. I keep tugging at the only two apertures

I have until finally, they droop so much that I can see, but now the mask is weeping. Where the mask sags, you can see my eyes, the deep brown skin that rings them. This becomes typical. The consequence of being seen is that you're seen. My parents, fearing that they will look like they bought me a crappy costume in front of the other parents, decide to scrap the mask altogether.

I sit war-paint still in the bathroom as my mother details in the web lines along my face, fills the red to blush between, drapes my eyelids with enough white. It's some of her finest work, and it's my favorite thing and the only thing I have ever seen her paint. I look in the mirror, and after this, the memory fades, but I need you to stay with me, here, in this moment for just a while longer. I want you to feel what I knew as I touched the drying paint and saw the long web over my mouth, my cheeks, stopping at my hairline. I want you to know I felt like a map to a city I'd never seen but always lived in. I want you to know I stood between my parents in the mirror, and I smiled until the paint nearly cracked. I returned to stand in front of the TV, hair blocking part of the view, an eclipse between skylines of pixels. I make for great expectations. I'm my parents' son. I'm Spider-Man, and I'm me. This is my universe, and everyone knows what I am. The mask is perfect because I am no longer underneath it.

OK, people, let's do this one more time. Spider-Man has always been Black, but he hasn't always been Spider-Man. This is the story of one Spider-Man in 2018, and in this universe, his name is Miles Morales. Peter Parker is dead, and Miles has gathered for the funeral with the rest of New York on a corner where, in my universe, my parents must have been in love once. Everyone is wearing masks, everyone is sad, the point is that anyone can wear the mask; everyone is counting on everyone to feel powerful, everyone is counting on everyone to be seen. The costume doesn't fit in the way most things don't fit in middle school, and we are told that it always fits eventually. Miles has been bitten, and Miles has his powers; he's Spider-Man, but not yet. The mask sags where his eyes are, and his brown skin is two perfect rings; he can see but doesn't know where to go. Everyone is counting on Miles, but only he knows it. In this way, we are the same boy, just in different universes.

I don't remember how old I was when the first person asked me, "What are you?" I know that the question must have come from somewhere. I know it's everywhere all the time. I know that Miles, like any of the boys we are, must wish, truly, that he was explaining one last time and could mean it. Origin stories are frustrating this way, a gravity we are pulled and pulled to; many Spider-Verses, but always the same series of violence.

So here's mine, for the sake of the story more than anything else. My father is Black and from St. Louis; though around strangers, he will say he is from Manhattan because sometimes we are from where we were least dead and not where we were born. My mother is Dominican and from Washington Heights, born and raised by parents who escaped the Trujillato. They've been alive together since the '80s—they've been alive together all my life. This is my origin as far as I can follow it: they met in New York and loved each other, and when I was born, they loved each other anywhere else but especially in Chicago. This is where I best like to remember them: as young and lucky as they will ever be in my memory, grief less legible on our faces than it is now.

Miles, similarly, is Black and Puerto Rican. Like me, he is made of questions, maybe most of all about his name. Miles's father is a Black man named Jefferson Davis. In this universe, he is voiced by Brian Tyree Henry with the tender weariness of a basset hound. In this way, he is familiar—he sounds like home in the best and worst ways. Miles's mother is a Puerto Rican woman named Rio Morales, voiced by Lauren Vélez, another language whispering beneath her few lines, a dance only shadows are fluent in. Like my mother, she is quiet, ever my father's translator even when everyone is speaking English. Every time I see them on screen, there we are—ourselves without ourselves.

There are a number of theories around the origin of Miles Morales's name. Like many speculations of how I came to be who and what I am, they range from "affirmative action" to "progress narrative." There are many Spider-Verses, and so there are many theories, but here's my favorite: Miles's father and his brother, Aaron, did a lot of dirt back before he was Miles's father. It was easiest to half-hide his son in the name of the woman he loved. I love this theory best because I am selfish. I was born into a country of no rain, so when it drizzles, I see a river; I see my face in every drop.

Reader, it's worth noting that I have gotten accustomed

to correcting my name because this is a blunt-tongued country. It's a heightened reflex, a sixth sense, an alarm always primed in my head—to smooth the *J* to an *H* in the mouths of the unfamiliar. It's not a hard name, I promise. I don't belong to a particularly tall sound, but I swing from it all the same. The origin story I was told is that my father wanted another *J,* my mother wanted something Spanish. They wanted a name that white people couldn't recognize as their son until I was already in the room. I am mispronounced by design, and it's sad but kind of funny. I am most Spider-Man when my oldest power was an accident. There is a me in every universe, and we are all tired of being invisible—we are all tired of disappearing. Obscurity is both an inheritance and a superpower; anybody indeed can wear the mask. Miles, I fear too few truly understand what it is to be born into it.

OK, people, let's do this one more time, Spider-Man has always been Black, but this time it's not the one you're thinking of. Before there was Miles Morales, there was Peter Parker. Before there was Peter Parker, there was Anansi, the Spider-Man. The first Spider-Man was a storyteller, the first storyteller. I learned this from my father, who read his origin to me every night. *A Story, A Story* is a children's book that tells the story of how Anansi, small and clever, outwitted the most dangerous creatures in the world to buy the stories of the world from the sky god Nyame. I didn't know then that this was how my father had managed to survive long enough to make me. My massive deep-voiced protector, reading to me from a book or spinning tales that I imagine he had been nursing all day in the back of his mind as he went through the motions of his corporate job.

At the mostly white school he sends me to, I do what children do: I mimic. I tell the story of the first Spider-Man and am met mostly with confusion. Spider-Man is white—everybody knows that. I grow quieter the older my small body becomes. I am invisible in stretches I can never predict. I try to turn them to my advantage anyway because this is what I know of power, better to be inside of it than against it. I negotiate, and I trick, and I pretend like my father, like Anansi. I learn to code-switch, not always when I want to but as some strange compromise between fight and flight. This camouflage becomes my voice—this mask becomes my face. I go to school in Chicago and Omaha and Philly and Minneapolis and always somewhere I don't belong, somewhere it is safer to not be me.

My parents are counting on me. Like Miles, they believe I am the best of all of them. Like Miles, all I want to do is escape back to what I know. I tell the story of Anansi then try, many times, to scale the fence at recess so I can sneak away, go home to where I am always seen, always loved. I fall each time because I don't have the strength to leave silence. I am a dark outline, a skyline of expectations happening to either side of my brief body. I am Spider-Man, but I'm not yet. I am me, but not quite. Parents ask more and more, *What are you?* I find ways to tell the story until I don't even notice how often in a day I use the word "half," I don't notice how much I believe it. I don't know the price of power, but I know that I want whatever can allow me to be away; whatever story is the price for that I chameleon into. Clever Boy, Clever Spider using his mouth to throw punches at the sky.

OK, people, let's do this one more time. Before Spider-Man was Spider-Man, he was a scholarship student. This is the story of two Spider-Men in 2018 and 2006, respectively. It's worth noting that I've never read *Great Expectations*, but I have been assigned more than a few essays to make sure I was as smart as advertised. In 2018 Miles Morales is on-screen and staring down the barrel of a zero-out-of-one-hundred score on a test. Before any more dialogue can pass, I know exactly what this is. Miles's teacher thinks she does, too, and says, "You're trying to quit, and I'm not going to let you." All the hairs on the back of my neck stand up, my sixth sense on red alert. Call it déjà vu or Spidey-Sense; call it memory or trigger. The end result is that I remember. Without my notice, my knuckles congeal into fists, my mouth goes dry because I have been here before. An Origin Story is another word for Beginning, for where we begin to learn. Lesson 1: Don't watch the mouth—watch the hands.

It is the winter of 2006 in Chicago when my history teacher tasks me with arguing in favor of slavery. He doesn't call it that, at first, but I know power when I see it. We are in one of my favorite rooms in the school, and despite what happened there, I'd be lying if I said I don't still have warm feelings toward some of it. Mr. Stone was a short white boy from Boston who kept a re-creation of the Last Supper where all of the disciples and Jesus himself are Black. I know this because I loved it, I know this because I stared at it because I couldn't look in his eyes as he hurt me. Months later, he will tell my father that he thinks I am trying to quit, but he's not going to let me.

We are in the room because I'm asking to be switched off the states' rights side of a civil war debate re-creation. My memory sputters when I remember whether there was another Black kid in the class or just me; what I remember is that I was the only one who was asked. Ordinarily, in class, I am quiet, I don't belong to a very tall sound, but I swing from it all the same as I all but beg him not to make me do this. I am not tall and, unknown to me at the time, never will be. I stand in the room with its warm lighting and the strange layering of decoration that can only happen if a teacher knows that they will leave the room when they choose and not before. Beyond the window in this universe, it is maybe snowing, and maybe not, the result is the same. My body is swimming in a graffiti Ecko Unltd. hoodie, a tiny Phat Farm chain that looks like it came out of an egg machine even though I spent all the money I had just to hold its shine for a bit, sits in my chest like an insignia. I flit in and out of visibility, my hair muzzled by a camouflage Chicago Bears hat I have been wearing every day since I started living only with my father while my mother attempts to sell our house from a failed move in Omaha. I have gotten good at pretending, I know to stare at someone's hair so it can be mistaken for eye contact, I notice Mr. Stone has my mother's hair while he tells me that arguing against slavery "wouldn't be enough of a challenge" for a student "like you."

Miles's teacher says that the only way for a person to get everything wrong is to know how to get everything right. I don't know if this is true. What I do know is that a week later, I am in class sitting behind a sign that says STATES' RIGHTS. I am dodging sneak attack after sneak attack as the pro-abolition group comes after me and not the other two kids on the panel, I grow quieter because I am trying to argue against myself. I flit in and out of visibility until Mr. Stone stops the debate and admonishes the class for not trying hard enough. I know he pointed to me and said, "Julian is up here arguing for slavery, what's your excuse for not trying?" Invisibility can be suffocating. Invisibility can be your only refuge. Like every refuge, invisibility can be taken away. The consequence of being seen is that you're seen.

The only way for a person to get everything wrong is to know how to get everything right. I don't know if this is true. But I know that as Chicago ballooned my Ecko jacket behind me and the suspicious eyes and sometimes bodies of cops trailed me through Lincoln Park as I walked farther north toward Lakeview and home that I was dressed like one expectation. *Julian is up here arguing for slavery, what's your excuse for not trying?* pulsed in my head as the outfit of a person I would never become rippled in the wind. I was not large enough for any of the expectations of my body and was somehow dying of all of them at once. Little eclipse around which a whole city is happening. I decide to start getting it wrong, to stop trying. If trying landed me arguing for my own destruction, if great expectations led me into such loneliness, then I wanted to be invisible for good. I watch my grades slip on purpose until even I believe it is because I am not equal to the work. I watch my classmates call me a half-breed—I don't know how to correct them because I have learned to assume that Half is my name.

Like Miles, in eighth grade, I was always somewhere I don't belong. Like Miles, I sometimes cursed my teachers' names the way Miles must curse the lottery ball that landed him where nothing seems to know how to love him. By that I mean, we curse the survival we were given off-screen. That America taught us we were invisible, and the only way for the invisible to punish those who refuse to see us is to first punish ourselves. Where some see a zero, we see a door. I never tell Mr. Stone that this was when I stopped trusting him. I smile and pretend everything is fine, and I tell him I just don't understand. I never tell him that sometimes I wonder what the difference is between wanting to quit and simply wanting to go home. This is my universe, and nobody knows what I am until it is time to punish me. I smile, I perform, I tell a story of how everything is fine. All my teachers know something is wrong—they don't know that they are what's wrong. The rest of the school year, my fists are knotted in my pockets until they cramp. Don't watch the mouth—watch the hands.

OK, people, let's do this one more time, Spider-Man has always been Black, but nobody knows who he is. I didn't hear the word "Afro-Latino" until I was already in college. By this time, I am nineteen and ragged, glitching in another universe that is not my own. It's harder to make friendships in the Latinx student group because I am learning again that I am a citizen of an old story, one where there are one or two ways to be "Latinx enough" and a multiverse of ways to be an exile. Despite the best efforts of an Afro-Latinx president, other students speak Spanish about me in front of me, as if I can't hear them. Because I admit I am not fluent, because I tell them I am not from either of the coasts but from Chicago, because my performance of Latinidad is inherently Black, because one of the Latinx students—a mentor of mine—starts nicknaming me "Blackface," maybe for all of these reasons or none of them, because they think I cannot understand them, I'm invisible again. Despite the best efforts of the Afro-Latinx president, this never changes, and nobody ever apologizes. In the few meetings I drag myself to, words like "We" and "Us" are thrown around, and I'd be lying to say it wasn't seductive, isn't still seductive, this notion of a "we." Wouldn't it be nice to have such a strong thread, a web that connected, a single story? "Us," "We," and "Nosotros" are words that shoot everywhere, thicken the air with laughter for a joke I'm not in on. Nobody says "anti-Blackness," they say racism as if it is not theirs too. Us, We, and Nosotros build a more elaborate web; the words are beautiful, but I am not allowed inside them.

We never see Miles have a crisis on-screen about being Black and Latinx. Never see him grinding his teeth at another "what are you?" This is one of my favorite parts of the movie, that Miles is always resolutely aware that he doesn't have to prove his Latinidad to anyone. I sometimes wonder if this is actually his least believable power.

It is "understood" for years in Latinx spaces that I am "(Insert person's) Black friend." This is true at every tour stop with my best friend, where the Latinx professors generally engage with him. It's true in every Latinx studies course I will take for the entirety of my undergraduate career. It's true when I say that there is a dangerous flattening of Latinx narratives in campus spaces when we treat Blackness as a disqualifier for Latinidad. It is true in the quiet that follows, the idle hands that stay idle.

It's not true. But you could have fooled me.

In reality, I have blood of my own—a mother and a language, and maybe the important thing to remember is that origin stories diverge depending on who is actually writing the story. Maybe the important thing to remember is that too often, the hands only look like my mother's. That there is no "we" until sweat is needed and whatever villains have always been at the door. Maybe the important thing to remember is that there are as many ways to be Latinx as there are Latinx people, that this is what it can mean when it is said that "anyone can wear the mask." Maybe the important thing to remember is that a web with only one line, one story is just a thread waiting to be cut. That as surely as there is a Spider-Man in every universe, the cut will always come.

Here's what I remember: the same night someone asks me if I am Afro-Latinx for the first time, I don't feel like a "half." Up until then, I had felt as if there were some crucial parts of being Latinx that I had gotten wrong, always slow on the draw to my own identity. Miles Morales has existed in my universe for a little over a year by this point, and because I want to hold on to this feeling I tweet out "#Julian4SpiderMan." I feel the mask slip over me, but it is my mask; it is "Us" enough for me.

OK, people, let's do this one more time. Spider-Man has always been Black, and part of being Spider-Man is that there are long silences between you and who you love. This is a story that starts like too many of my stories. I'm depressed in my dorm room, ignoring a call from my dad until it goes to voicemail. Every bed I'm in feels as though I have been tied to it. No matter how I enter a room, it feels as though I have been left behind in it. I would say it's an ungodly hour, but anyone who's been depressed knows that, in the midst of an episode, they are all ungodly hours.

I don't have the strength to leave silence, and silence has no interest in leaving me. How do you explain to someone you love how often your greatest nemesis lives in your head? That sometimes it feels as though you are the mask? That it has been such a long time since you heard yourself speak that you're not sure what your voice sounds like anymore, that past a certain point even sounds become invisible? That it can be like this for weeks, that a month all but disappears and you don't know how?

For most of *Spider-Verse*, Miles's parents have no idea where he is. He is a citizen of an old story like I am. The son believing that whatever is changing in him is too much danger for his family to bear—the parents believing the most dangerous change is how easily their boy inflicts his invisibility on them. Miles's father leaves message after message; they stack and blink in Miles's phone as they did in mine, cluttered like love or mail for a man who's something like dead. The unfortunate thing about becoming powerful is that you become acquainted all over again with what it feels like to be treated like a problem. No matter who you save, you realize that you will always be a problem to somebody.

An interesting thing about *Spider-Verse* is that Miles Morales is slow by design. Miles is initially animated at twelve frames per second, unlike nearly everything else in his world, which moves at a standard twenty-four frames per second. Depression feels like this to me, as if the world is happening faster than I can conceive of moving to catch up to it. How many versions of the world passed while I listened to the phone buzz as if it were on the other side of the door? Heard the invariable pattern of my father finding new ways to say, "I'm worried"? It goes like this for years, two boys searching beneath the door for each other's shadows, for proof something is moving.

The order of my father's voicemails never changes. It's one of the innumerable things I love about him. He always starts, "Hey Julian, it's your dad," as if he is not the only person who still leaves me voicemails. He tells me, even when I have disappeared for days, weeks, that he is proud of me, that I am his son. I try not to forget to be grateful for these when the world is moving faster than I have the strength to—I forget anyway sometimes. I am telling you all of this so that you know that when Miles's father says, "I see this spark in you, it's amazing, it's why I push you; but it's yours, whatever you choose to do with it, you'll be great." No matter where I am, it is 2015 again. I am standing on a street corner in Philly, and my father tells me, "I am sorry if I have failed you. No matter who you want to be, I know you'll be the best at it. I love you. Nothing will ever stop that, do you believe me?"

How long had the danger been building in me that I could let him think I could ever forget that?

In the theater, I am crying, and it is 2018. In 2015, I felt a prick behind my eyes, like tears but none fall. I have no witness, but stay with me here for a second—let's imagine my eyes ringed by an energy I must master to learn how to save people, let's imagine what I remember: that this is the moment I began to learn how to save myself, that it is, above all else, a leap of faith.

OK, people, let's do this one last time. Sometimes the only cure for danger is to become more dangerous. Reader, I, too, have emerged from invisibility with a spark loose in my hands. In my saddest hours, I have looked at the window and told myself a hundred stories about falling, and I am so sorry that I once courted danger this way. But stay with me here for a second—I'm saying a new origin story, and I know that I've earned it. Miles in his universe is where I have dreamed myself too often suspended between skyline and ground, pulling the window behind me, each shard making a sky full of daggers. Afro-Latinx life is this in so many ways, to be taught that you are dangerous and shameful and difficult to imagine; yet here we are floating like always—

dragging the mirror of the window until it breaks, making the space between alive with our unmistakable light.

I have a confession: I love this scene but have only ever seen it all the way through once despite watching *Spider-Verse*, at a conservative estimate, twenty-two times. I close my eyes in the middle every time. And it's because being Afro-Latinx means that there are times where your only government is where the drums yield to a voice. It is the moment that Miles hurtles, eyes narrowing, toward the ground. It is the moment where the boy we were becomes something constant across all universes.

Faith is a slippery word. I have lived much of my life not knowing what it means and being disappointed in its uses. But there's a moment at exactly 1:24:06, where Miles's web connects to the building he leapt from, and the body jerks into another kind of flight. It's the moment right after this where I close my eyes each time and call out alongside Blackway, "Can't stop me now!" And I don't know much about faith, but I know it feels like that. Being Afro-Latinx is many things, but I know it feels like this. And maybe it is the irony that I love best, that I see myself best sometimes with my eyes closed and a song beckoning danger, how I know the drums in my blood and know the boy will rise each time.

The moment Miles Morales becomes Spider-Man is more than the end to a hero's journey. It is more than representation. Each time I watch it, I am gifted back to myself: Spider-Man in a hoodie and Jordans, Spider-Man in the city where my parents fell in love, Spider-Man in the place where none of us died—where one universe split from another and yet we wear mostly the same mask, mostly the same face. The voices that follow him as he swings into his new life, into full command of his powers, are the voices of my family. Representation matters, but this is more than that. It is one thing to have spent too much of life begging to be seen, relying on cowardly love and finding it beneath my own tongue when I described myself as "half Latinx, half Black." It is another thing entirely to finally imagine myself, mid-leap, all the noise of a city below me and expect, finally, to live.

Miles pulls the mask from his face to reveal his face, and I am six again. Spider-Man's face is my face, and I remember, finally at age twenty-six, that it has always been this way. On opposite sides of the screen, we are both wearing the half-grins of someone who could have died but didn't. We exist, and there is no need to explain, and this is my favorite love song. Spider-Man has always been Black, and we're not half of anything.

Half In, Half Out
ORBITING A WORLD FULL OF PEOPLE OF COLOR
Saraciea J. Fennell

When you were born, you cried and the world
rejoiced. Live your life so that when you die,
the world cries and you rejoice.
—CHEROKEE PROVERB

When I was born, I came out red.

The way my mother tells it, I came out blood orange. I'm not sure what the doctors thought as they looked up at my parents: a Black man as dark as the inside of an endless pit, with slick wavy hair fit for an Indio, and a brown woman with thin, penciled-in lines for eyebrows and thick black corkscrew curls.

After they cleaned me up and the hospital air hit my lungs, my skin turned white. Yes, I know what you're thinking: How can that be? I ask my mother the same thing. "Tell me again how I came out," I'll ask at random. Each time there's a new detail: "You looked so much like your father's mother—she was Native from the South," or, "A head full of hair you had, it was dark and bone straight, with a curl at the ends." Even my tiny fingers were white, but there were traces of color around the nail beds, dark halos around my earlobes, hints for what my skin would eventually become—brown.

I think about that a lot.

I grew up in a family where complexions varied like bruised and unripe fruit. We never thought to question why our skin is a particular color—my older sister Nina, light-skinned with a green undertone, my sister Jaime, light-skinned with more yellow and pink undertones. My brother and I—everyone swears that we are twins—both brown until sun-kissed when our tanned skin becomes the color of an eclipse. Hair as textured as they come, at times more coil than curl, at others more fine than coarse. All six of us so very different, but still familia no matter what.

Some family members spoke Spanish, especially the elders, like my tías, who only communicated in español, but all of my siblings and primos spoke English. It was normal for us to speak to the elders in English and them back to us in their native tongue. And if you didn't understand the language, you learned to pay attention to the body because facial expressions and hand gestures spoke volumes. A flick of the hand and the phrase "déjalo" meant leave it alone; knitting of the eyebrows, concerned eyes, tilt of the head, with a hand on the shoulder and "ya comiste?" meant have you eaten yet. It's strange to not speak a language fluently yet still be attuned to its meaning, but it's comforting all the same.

Back in Brooklyn, East New York, where I was born and raised, everyone in the projects was either Black, African, or Latinx. Having only been surrounded by people of color, I thought that's what the rest of the world must look like. Imagine my surprise when my younger sister and I ended up in foster care at the ages of five and eight, plucked from the hood into an affluent part of Brooklyn to live with a middle-aged married white couple. They had a nice house, with an upstairs and a basement. It was probably the first time in my life where I had to sit at the dining room table for every freaking meal.

My sense of the world changed rapidly, and because I was a keen observer as a kid, I quickly learned all the ways that I stood out from white people. Hair perceived too wild to be tamed by the untrained hands of a white woman (thank God my mother taught me how to gather my mane into a ponytail). Requesting arroz con pollo, casamiento, a staple in my family's household, only to be given chicken noodle soup and a sandwich. Attending a school where an annoying white boy talked on and on about how he and his dad traveled to fancy museums around the city and the Brooklyn Botanical Garden all the time. At first, I was intrigued, devoured his stories like sprinkles on ice cream until his life started to seem too glamorous for me. I was only eight but had never been to the botanical garden or a museum. Most importantly, though, he had access to his family, and I did not, and that hurt. So the next time he droned on and on in class about riding the train into the Bronx with his dad to visit the New York Botanical Garden, I snapped on him. I begged for him to shut up and keep his stories to himself, but he just turned over his shoulder and kept on talking to the next student, unfazed.

I hated school. It was just another building, another

mostly white space where I felt out of place. I didn't want to go—but I didn't want to stay at home with my foster parents either. Teachers encouraged me to try to make friends. Regular check-ins with the guidance counselor, questions from my foster mom about how school was going, missing my family something fierce—too many emotions washed over me—anxiety, sadness, but more than anything anger, so I kept to myself.

I had convinced myself family was all I needed and that my mom was coming to rescue us at any moment. Every day after school, I looked forward to when the phone rang because I knew it would be Mami calling. I'd sit on the sofa drumming my feet against the base listening to Mami tell me how she was working on getting us all back together. How I had to be on my best behavior—cuidarse— look out for my younger sister, don't just trust anyone or let anyone touch us inappropriately.

Mami filled me up with her empty promises to come to scoop us up. Her calls became less frequent, and I finally stopped believing her.

I found myself eager to connect with a community that looked like me. But it was hard as a transfer student in the middle of the school year. While my white classmates could easily sucker the attention of my peers, I could not. After weeks of isolation and unsuccessful attempts at making friends, my teacher partnered me up with one of the other Black girls in class for an assignment. It was the greatest thing that could've happened to me. We became fast friends. Suddenly I was eager to go to school because I had something to look forward to. Someone to share secrets with.

We hung out all the time—sat next to each other in class, during lunch; at recess, we chased each other around the yard and played jump rope and tag. She even introduced me to a few of her friends and other kids of color.

Everyone started to think we were related—at the time, I thought it was because of how much time we were spending together, but now that I'm older, I know that it was just white people confusing us. Like when I showed up to class late from lunch one time and was called by her name instead of my own. The white teacher swore that I was her, but when I reminded her that my friend was actually not in school that day, she just clucked her tongue and said that she would be sure to mark me present. Things like that happened frequently. People would have a hard time calling me by my name, so Saraciea was folded into Shanice because her name was easier to pronounce. When she or I corrected them, folks just laughed it off, never really apologizing; they'd shrug their shoulders and blame it on us looking alike and sounding alike. Teachers claimed it was because we were inseparable.

Despite all of that, I finally started to feel like things were going to be okay, that I belonged again, that I could maybe survive being away from my family because I was no longer orbiting the world alone.

My world shattered all over again when I was told that I would be removed from the white foster family's home and placed in the Bronx with my tía and her family. It's not like I wasn't excited about being reunited with familia—it was more so the look on my friend's face when I broke the news that I was leaving. She asked me where I was moving to, and I told her, and then she asked if it was because I was a foster kid. I'd never told her that I was in the system—my guess was the teachers probably did. Just like that, her words made me question if what we shared was even real or if she was just taking pity on me like everyone else.

The day I left the foster family's home is a complete blur, but I still remember that huge wooden dining room table, that sofa where my tiny body imprinted every day as I sat biting my nails, gnawing on the inside of my lip and cheek until they were raw, waiting for the phone to ring just to speak to my mom, and sometimes my other siblings—three-way was truly our saving grace. Most of all, I will always remember that white woman's face when we arrived on her doorstep in the middle of the night, with her wire-rimmed glasses perched on the brim of her nose. She was so patient with me, even when I lashed out in anger. Screaming how I didn't want to be there and for the social worker to take us back to Mami.

We met Mami and tía in a secluded family room in some tall building in downtown Manhattan. We frequently traveled into the city thanks to my being in the system; it's where we went to meet with our caseworker, and on rare occasions where my sister and I would have supervised visits with Mami. My other sister, Jaime, and cousins were in that room waiting for us. I swear I was so excited that I felt my heart pounding in my fingertips. Even though I would still technically be in the foster care system, we were all happy to be among family again. It made being away from my brothers and sisters and Mami better because we weren't surrounded by strangers or gringos. Plus, we could call each other at any time, and my mom could pop over to see us whenever she wanted.

We moved into Tía's house with quickness—we didn't have much luggage to begin with, so it was easy to get settled. All six of my siblings were there that first night, so it was a reunion of sorts. Nina had come all the way from Brooklyn to see us, my sister Jaime was already living with Titi, and my brothers had transferred from the group home into her custody too. We ate a traditional Latin home-cooked meal, and then the fifteen of us piled up in the living room, some of us on the sofa, the kids on the floor listening to Mami, Titi, and my older siblings tell us stories about everything that had transpired while we were split apart. We talked for hours on end until the younger kids fell asleep, until Mami and my sister had to say goodbye to go back to Brooklyn. Nina promised she'd visit again, and Mami promised that we would all be back home real soon.

My tío, whom everyone called Papo, was the best uncle, hands down. He was Puerto Rican with German roots, so all of my cousins were various shades of brown but also white. You'd never know my cuz—a white Latina—pale skin, long dirty blonde hair, and everything, was Puerto Rican and Honduran unless you knew her last name, heard her speak Spanish, or spotted her with her parents. But you'd also never suspect that I—with darker skin and long thick curly frizzy brown hair—was Latina either. As kids, we had no reason to question our identity, but society forced us to. Because I stood out from the rest of my cousins, I was singled out a lot. An easy target for people to pick at when it came to our mixed race family. It seemed as though everyone was armed and ready to challenge my right to exist. First, it was I couldn't be Black because my hair was too "nice"—I had that "good hair" according to all of the Black kids at my new school, in this new beast of a borough—the Bronx. I suddenly had to be "mixed" or "Spanish," Puerto Rican, or Dominican. I couldn't just be Black. I had to be *mixed* with something—and half the time, I didn't even know what being mixed meant. I mean, honestly, what nine-year-old is concerning herself with that?

I'll never forget that one day, my cousin—who is two years older—and I were playing Double Dutch in front of her beat-up Section 8 house on Allerton and Wallace Avenue when one of her friends asked to join us. We were excited to have someone else man the rope instead of using the gate to help us turn. But instead of just joining us, she asked who I was and where I came from. As if I was some outsider, some stranger who didn't belong. Of course, my cuz and I both responded that I was her cousin from Brooklyn and that I would be living with them now. That should've deaded the conversation right there, but instead, she probed on. "Okay, cool, but how is that your cousin if she's darker than you? Is she Puerto Rican too?"

My throat closed up as I scowled at the girl and gripped the rope tighter. Who was she to call me out like that? I was so taken aback I didn't know how to respond. Neither did my cuz. This was all new to me. I had no idea at that age what it meant to be Puerto Rican. All I knew was that I was Black, and that was that. But there we were having this conversation when I was just trying to kick it with my cousin and jump some rope. My cousin fidgeted with the rope in her hands, shifting her weight around. It felt like we were trapped in that moment forever until my cousin finally just blurted, "Yeah, she the same thing as me, Puerto Rican and Hondurian." At the time, I believed if my older cuz said we were the same, then we were the same, punto final. I didn't even pick up at the time that she said "Hondurian" instead of Honduran, which later on in life a Honduran friend would correct me on—I had spent what felt like a lifetime mislabeling myself. My cousin's answer did the trick though because the girl shrugged it off like nothing, grabbed the rope, and introduced herself to me. The weirdness I felt dissipated, and we started jumping rope again.

That moment rocked me to my core, but it simultaneously empowered me. I had been navigating the world not really knowing anything about my culture, or where I came from. It made me take stock of who I was and who my family was too. It's not like I was learning about Honduras in school, so I found I needed to find a way to get answers on my own. I started to pay closer attention to everything and everyone. I secretly questioned why we did certain things, from the way we wore our hair to the food we ate and the holidays we celebrated. I even started to associate being Puerto Rican with being Black.

When Black kids at school cornered me on the playground, in the lunchroom, or during physical education and asked me what my ethnicity was, I stuck out my chest, stood upright, and proudly told them I was Puerto Rican and Honduran. It felt good finally claiming my identity, but I also paid attention to how their faces changed.

How some would be excited that I was suddenly not just another Black girl, but also Hispanic, and others a little defeated that I didn't answer just Black.

The kids I considered friends were friends just because I liked them; it wasn't about race or ethnicity. But I did notice how Latinx kids began to embrace me. Suddenly they felt like they had a claim on me. I'd walk onto the schoolyard waiting for us to line up to go inside the school, and they'd approach me, all smiles and high fives like we had been BFFs all along. Commenting on my hair, and sharing thoughts like, "I knew you had to be Spanish because there's something about your complexion, like you look exotic." What made things even stranger is everyone knew my cousins. Once they found out that I was related to them, people were nicer to me: not just the Latinx and Black kids, but the popular kids too.

Even though we were two years apart, my prima seemed so tapped into things about our culture, about the world, whereas I felt like I had no clue. We spent so much time together while I lived with my aunt. We did everything together. We both rocked slicked-back ponytails and messy buns. We were partners in crime, from stealing sips of Corona behind Tío Papo's back to pocketing coins from Titi's laundry money.

Titi made us buy the same things and wear our hair the same way. She was very much equal, equal until she wasn't. For some strange reason, even though my cousin and I were close, we clashed *a lot*. She hated that I was in her shadow, following her everywhere, even when she snuck out to kiss her secret boyfriend. It became apparent that even though I believed with my whole heart that we were the same, we definitely were not.

The way Western culture, and, especially, American culture, shames us for being non-white is heartbreaking. When I was younger, Mami would either braid my hair, put it in nudos—Bantu knots—or, my least favorite, use the hot comb. But while living with Tía, she and my sister Jaime decided my hair needed to be straight and more manageable, so they put a relaxer in my hair—JUST FOR ME is what the box said. I was about nine, and the thought of having silky straight hair like the beautiful Black girl on the box made my insides burst with excitement. I won't lie—it was the most painless of all the hairstyling sessions aside from my scalp tingling here and there. I remember sitting on the floor between my sister's legs as she parted my hair in four sections, greased my edges and my kitchen. She draped a towel over my shoulders, put on the noisy plastic gloves, and started applying the chemical straightener to my hair. I wasn't allowed to run around and play with my cousins. I had to sit and wait for the relaxer to take. That thirty minutes felt like a lifetime as my hair went from curly to wavy to straight. Periodically, I'd sneak into the bathroom, close the door, and stare at myself as my hair transformed. Not yet realizing that the seeds of self-hatred were being sown as the minutes ticked on.

Once the time was up, my sister and I went to the bathroom to wash it out. Both of us on our knees hunched over the tub washing the product from my hair. When I emerged, and in front of the mirror, I barely recognized myself. I had never seen my hair wet and so straight. It was so long too. As a tomboy, I mainly wore my hair in a ponytail, but this new hair made me feel more beautiful.

When I was older, though, I resented having had my hair relaxed. I often wonder what my original hair texture was like back then. Even though I've had natural hair since I was a junior in high school, I still feel like it never returned to what it once was.

Relaxing my hair wasn't the only anti-Black/Western ideals thing that was consciously imparted to me as a kid. Anytime one of us got hurt, we were instructed to use bleaching cream to take away or minimize the scarring. But for me (and any of my darker-skinned siblings or cousins), using bleaching cream on my knees and elbows was part of my daily ritual. We were instructed to apply the bleaching cream on any dark spots—one of my cousins even put it on her face. Honestly, looking back now, I know that it was just my family being anti-Black and navigating colorism. It's part of the hard truths we've had to grapple with. We've always celebrated our Blackness, our African and Indigenous roots, but deep down inside, we were all dealing with our own self-hate that was driven by what society and the media told us constantly—the closer you can get to whiteness, the better your life will be. Even now, until this day, I have to check my sisters, my cousins, and especially my mom, who still makes comments about my hair and what's acceptable to her. I politely remind her of all the ways she is contributing to white, Western ideals.

As I got older, I continued to ask questions about my family's ancestry. I desperately needed to know what our roots were so I could dictate my identity—not other people. Through conversations with my mother, I finally learned that I was, in fact, *not* Puerto Rican—that was my cousin's identity. I was, in fact, Black, Native American, Honduran, and Garifuna.

My mother and I have had extensive discussions about what it was like when she arrived in the States as a young girl, and one thing she told me has always struck a chord with me. She and the rest of her Honduran siblings were told to identify as Honduran, as Hispanic, never as Black because of the way they would be treated. That, for me, just hit different as I matured and navigated the world. Everyone is conditioned to view Black people as if we don't matter. Even among the Black community, society finds ways to pit us against each other, from colorism to the critiquing of our hair, our bodies, and so forth.

It was refreshing to have something to say whenever people asked me what I was, where I was from. I took so much pride in saying, "I'm Hondureña—my mom is from Honduras." And then more questions would come. What part of Honduras was she from? La Ceiba—we are Indias y Negras, we trace our heritage from the women. While other kids my age knew who they were, where they came from, I was only beginning to scratch the surface. I felt as though I had been robbed. You see, my grandmother ran away from her family when they moved from Honduras to the Bronx in the 1960s. Because of that, my mother and her siblings didn't grow up in a traditional Honduran household. Instead, my grandfather raised them, but he was always away working on ships, so he enlisted neighbors whom he trusted to look after them. Those neighbors were Black and Puerto Rican, so we definitely have their influences in our upbringing. I can eat arroz con pollo with mac and cheese and collard greens and then have flan for dessert. Our home was a melting pot.

I'm still actively uncovering the history and ancestry of my family. The elders in the family clam up whenever I start poking around, digging through family photos, asking questions about family members, about our dirty and shameful family secrets. Nobody ever talks to me if we are in a large group, but I've cornered my first cousins, and they spill the tea. I follow up with my tías, so many tías, who all hold a different piece of the puzzle when it comes to family history. Slowly but surely, I am capturing and low-key recording my findings so that others who have questions won't have to dig so deep to uncover our truth. So much has been lost purposefully over the years. I can trace my father's roots back to the white plantation owners in the South from his last name—Fennell—and though I know it's just a name, it carries all that history and pain. I'm focused on my Honduran side of the family at the moment. I imagine my father's history will be much more painful for me to explore, and I'm not sure I'm ready to go there just yet.

But I finally truly have a sense of who I am, a Black, Indigenous, Honduran woman. And I vow to never deny parts of myself for anyone, but instead to lean in, plant roots, and let the history of my ancestors live on through me by sharing what I've learned about us with my son and my future children. I'm proactively having conversations with my siblings and discussing things about our childhood, how we were raised and the things that society forced on us so that we don't make the same mistakes with our own children. I've invested the time in explaining to the young people in my family that they can be more than one thing no matter what the world dictates, no matter what other Black or Latinx people tell them. Only we can tell the world who we are, but first, we must learn where we come from.

Haitian Sensation
Ibi Zoboi

The first time someone called me a Haitian booty scratcher was in elementary school. I don't remember what grade, but it was in the eighties at the height of the HIV/AIDS epidemic, a disease that the Center for Disease Control blamed Haitians for. When the world was searching for answers about an ominous virus that was ravaging developing countries in Africa and the Caribbean and the gay and trans communities in the United States, the CDC created what was then called the 4Hs. It stated that someone could contract HIV/AIDS by being a hemophiliac, a heroin user, a homosexual, or Haitian.

I was twelve when Haitians in New York City marched across the Brooklyn Bridge to protest the CDC. By then, the damage had already been done. I could never get the image out of my head—that of a random Haitian scratching their butt. I was too young to understand the layers of offense in that one statement. It meant that we were inherently diseased. This idea was backed by the media and a government institution.

No one wanted to be Haitian when I was growing up in Brooklyn, New York. There were plenty of Haitian immigrants, but the lifesaving answer to the pervasive question, "You Haitian?" was usually, "No!" Or better yet, "Hell no!" Even with our very Haitian names and our thick accents, some of us said this with our chests out, proudly. But to anyone who recognized all the markers of Haitianness, the follow-up statement would be, "Well, you *look* Haitian."

Haitianness definitely had a look. As a little girl, I wore ribbons in my hair to match my outfits. My many bobos and barrettes were stored in a cookie tin. You know the ones—the blue and gold metal tins that stored Danish butter cookies. Caribbean and Latinx immigrants never threw away that tin box. Haitians kept it for hair accessories, of which I had plenty. In my Bushwick neighborhood of Brooklyn, there were Puerto Ricans, Dominicans, Panamanians, Jamaicans, and Black Americans. None of them had as many hair accessories as I did. So every morning on my way to school, I'd unclip a barrette, untie a ribbon, pull some of my hair out of a bobo and make myself a bang. This was how I learned to assimilate—through hair.

Since there weren't any white kids in Bushwick (maybe a few Italian kids got mistaken for Puerto Rican), the girls with the longest hair in my classes were Dominican and Puerto Rican. In the second grade, Amarlise Gonzalez had the longest hair. She wore it in two braids that seemed to reach the back of her knees. I was obsessed with long hair. Back then, white women wore their hair down their backs like Cher, and all I wanted to do was run my fingers through those silky strands. And that's exactly what I did when I would sit behind Amarlise in class. She'd toss one of those long braids back, and it would land on my desk. I would bring a small comb to school, and I'd blissfully undo and redo her braid.

But our teacher, Sister Mary, caught me and separated us. She made me sit behind Anna, who was Puerto Rican and was the whitest-looking girl in the class with her light hair and eyes. This was even better. Anna wore her dirty blonde hair loose. But when Anna felt me messing with her hair, she turned around and gave me the meanest Puerto Rican evil eye (which is not as bad as the Haitian evil eye or the Jamaican evil eye, but still). Anna, the teacher's pet, told Sister Mary, who made me sit at the front of the class, behind no one.

Though I didn't have the vocabulary for it then, that's when I began to understand the proximity to whiteness. We were all Black and Latinx kids, but some of those Brown kids could pass for white, and I noticed how they were rewarded for it. The longer the hair, the lighter the eyes and skin, the closer they were to our white teacher, and thus, power.

By fifth grade, I understood the pecking order in our class, and, naturally, I tried to find a way to fit into this hierarchy. I noticed who was at the very bottom—the Black boys and girls with the darkest skin. There was this one Jamaican boy who would always get sent to the office. There was another dark-skinned girl who the nuns would always yell at. She had hair like mine—two short, stiff pigtails that stood straight out of each side of her head. Sometimes her bang would be curled around a pink sponge roller that she kept in all day. For some reason, I don't remember her name. But I remember Anna, Amarlise, Maria, Yasmine, and all the other Puerto Rican and Dominican girls who had power in that Bushwick classroom. The teachers sent them on errands (this was the ultimate power) and called on them when they raised their hands. The boys sent them love notes, and they were the first to have boyfriends.

I felt invisible until I started to hang with Anna and Amarlise and their crew. When one of them asked me, "You Spanish?" I said, "Sí!" I went on to explain that Pascale was actually short for Pascalena because I'm Dominican. I wasn't totally lying. There was no harm in adding a couple of letters to my name. Plus, Haiti and the Dominican Republic were on the same island, so it was practically one nation. I mean, it once was. They let me hang with them but on the sidelines, like a cheerleader. Sometimes I'd go chill with the few other Haitian girls and the Jamaican girls just to see what I was missing. But nothing could compare to me and Amarlise's love for curly-haired Puerto Rican boys, Gitano Eva Joia jeans, and Menudo. I passed for Spanish with my perfected "Mira, ven acá!" I got my first relaxer when I turned ten, and from then, it was a wrap. With my newly straightened hair, you couldn't tell me that I wasn't a Dominicana. My home life, filled with Haitian Creole, news of a failing dictatorship in Haiti, and memories of anti-Haitian politics in the Dominican Republic, was pushed aside to not only assimilate into American culture but to fit into Bushwick's Latinx community.

That didn't last, of course, because identity has a way of calling you back to your true self. We moved out of Bushwick after elementary school. I was in Queens now, in a much more diverse public middle school. There were few Latinx kids, and the social hierarchy now included Asian, South Asian, and Greek kids. Hair was no longer a form of power. It was intelligence. I was placed in a Gifted & Talented class and was the only Black girl there. Claiming to be Spanish would not get me any closer to power.

For high school, I was back at a Catholic institution. My mother bought a house in a Black middle-class neighborhood, and we were closer to the American Dream now, worlds away from Bushwick and the crack and HIV/AIDS epidemics. With only twenty Black kids (of which half were Haitian and were some of my closest friends) in a graduating class of seven hundred, assimilation into any culture other than my own would be a major transgression. This was an elite school, and the girls who spoke Spanish were also Colombian, Peruvian, and Ecuadorian. They were not the ones with power, and they would not have let me into their tight-knit circle anyway. Here, proximity to whiteness was actually being white. My social climbing tactics from elementary school wouldn't work in a space where Irish and Italian kids wielded actual power based on generational wealth. My perfect "Mira, ven acá!" made no sense in my Spanish honors class where my classmates had actually been to Spain.

By this time, my love for Menudo shifted to New Edition and then to Jodeci and all the other boy groups in the nineties. Conscious hip-hop from A Tribe Called Quest and Arrested Development was my personal soundtrack. Black boys with dreads, leather bombers, and Timbs were now checking for me. Blackness was an identity I could be fully immersed in without being relegated to the cultural sidelines. I rocked a short haircut, and the mirrors around me were all the other girls with that same hairstyle. No one asked me if I was Spanish, and by the time the Fugees dropped their first album, my answer to being Haitian was a proud and resounding, "Hell yeah!"

It was a long journey to get here, one that included more positive Haitian representation in the media, pushing back against microaggressions in my predominantly white school, witnessing state-sanctioned violence against Black boys and misogyny and assault against Black girls and women. I also learned about the Haitian revolution, Vodou, and African history. Over the years, I realized that what I was trying to connect with in elementary school was a certain island flavor that resembled home. Haiti was colonized by the French. French, along with Spanish, Italian, and Portuguese, are Latin-based romance languages. So any Indigenous or African people in the New World colonized by Latin countries are considered to be part of Latin America. Technically, Haiti is part of Latin America.

There is music in everything about our shared culture. Salsa and merengue rhythms echo in Haitian compas. While Haitians have rara music, Dominicans have gaga—a street procession that includes whistles, maracas, güiros, and bamboo horns. Even the foods are fusions of our collective African, Arawak, and Taino lineage influenced by French and Spanish cuisine. This was what I remembered in my Bushwick neighborhood. The smell of bacalao coming out of Dominican and Puerto Rican apartments on Saturday mornings was also mori in my Haitian home. Of course, plantains in all their delicious forms are universal across most of Latin America. Hair politics aside, food, music, and culture were ways of folding myself into some memory of my home culture without the constraints of racist epithets and negative imagery in the media.

Despite these many cultural threads that link one Latin American nation to another, Haiti never claimed to be something other than African. We are Neg Mawon—maroons who snatched our freedom from the clutches of slavery, escaped to the mountains and plotted a revolution. Of course, there are some of us who inch closer to whiteness with our skin, hair, wealth, and personal politics. But as I got older and the world and its many layers of lies and truths opened up to me, I wanted nothing more than to claim Blackness as a way to anchor my soul to something truly powerful.

There is no denying Haiti's African roots. While there are many racially ambiguous Haitians living in the country and throughout the diaspora, Haitians are Black people. But outside of American racial politics, Blackness in Haiti is simply Africanness. It's in our skin, bones, and blood. It's in our language, music, and food. One of Haiti's most famous dishes is black rice. It's made by cooking rice in the thick, rich black water produced by dried mushrooms. There is also callaloo and tomtom—okra stew and pounded breadfruit that is reminiscent of the fufu and okra dishes found across West Africa.

It's only recently that the term Afro-Latin has become part of our collective vocabulary. When I was growing up, it was simply Spanish. Then, it was Hispanic. Now, the

Afro- prefix allows room for Latin Americans to claim an African or Black identity. Much like Puerto Rican Anna being the "whitest" girl in my class, the media has mostly portrayed the whitest parts of Spanish-speaking countries. Haiti, on the other hand, has never had that representation, despite the fact that there are certainly white-passing Haitians. When I was trying to pass as "Spanish" as a little girl, I was identifying with the Black Dominicans who were also in my class and in my neighborhood—the ones who I could've sworn were simply Black, but their island Spanish would come out as thick as polenta. I connected with that part of being "Spanish." It was a bilingual island flavor without the baggage that came with Haitian Creole, which is a mix of African, Indigenous, and French words.

Oftentimes the question that follows whether or not I am Haitian is, "You do voodoo?" And my answer to that is now a resounding and confident, "Yes!" American media has always portrayed Vodou in a negative light. However, I know that African culture is a patchwork quilt laid across Latin America. This quilt is made up of Candomblé in Brazil, Palo in Cuba, Santería or Lukumi in Puerto Rico, and Vodou in Haiti. Those ancestors and deities never left us. We've folded them into Catholicism because the saints and the orishá or lwa are in conversation.

Now, no one asks me if I am an Afro-Latina. I'm simply invited to sit at the table. I don't mind at all. I welcome it. This is a gesture that recognizes anti-Blackness in the Latinx community, especially among Dominicans who have long denied their Haitian connection. If I, as a Haitian, can be included in the conversations surrounding Afro-

Latinidad, then Black Dominicans can begin to claim their African heritage. Central and South America can also acknowledge the Garifuna of Guatemala and the Quilombos of Brazil—communities that rejected cultural annihilation and held on to the culture of their African ancestors.

I am proud to be a part of a movement that recognizes and honors the part of ourselves that colonialism tried so hard to eradicate. However, if anyone asks me now if I am an Afro-Latina, I will proudly say no, I am not. This is something I had to write through. I had to figure out my identity once again. I don't want to have to reconsider my position simply because new words have been added to our collective vocabulary. Others acknowledging the truth of their identities does not change what I've been all along and what the world has seen all along. I am Black. I am African. I am Haitian. Simply claiming a Haitian identity includes my birth country's long and troubled history with France, its colonizer. It's a history that is in my bones and blood. I am also culturally American. It's an existence I can't deny either. Though what grounds me in all these intersections in my identity is that I am Black and African first, whether it's in America, Latin America, or Haiti. It's what the world sees, and it's what I know and feel and remember.

The Land, the Ghosts, and Me

Cristina Arreola

El Paso is dry and dusty most of the year, with mountains that sprout from the earth like spiny tortoises, with few trees or bushes as adornment, only cacti brushing along their brown shells. It's a strange and uncanny beauty—a place that could only exist in the realm between the living and the dead and between two countries. When I think of El Paso, I think of the land, and I think of the ghosts.

My father and I always knew there was something in the land of West Texas that existed before us, beside us, and after us. There were shadows and memories that stamped places with their energy and left echoes in the universe. My mother never saw or felt them, but she never doubted them either. She told me I had a "strawberry" mark on the top of my spine, a physical representation of a spiritual gift: I could see the things that others couldn't. It meant that I could sense the ghosts that brushed at our ankles as we stood in the kitchen or came to whisper at my neck as I played in the den. I could feel the ghosts that sent me running in the night to the comfort of my parents' room, where I stood at the foot of the bed, scared to wake them but too scared to be alone.

"Just ask them to leave," my father told me on the nights when I couldn't sleep. "And they'll go."

But it wasn't that simple. "They don't speak like you and me, so you have to think it more than say it," my father said. What kept the ghosts from hearing my thoughts? What if they could hear them all? What if they could use my worst fears against me? After being awoken by spirits in the dead of night, I would run from my bedroom, through the den, and into the pantry. I would rummage through drawers until I found a cloudy plastic bottle filled with Holy Water—a relic from the days when we attended church more regularly. I would douse my fingers in the liquid and sign the cross on my body before running back to my room, where I would sleep with the covers above my head and silently pray under my breath for dawn to break.

We didn't celebrate the Mexican traditions that might have put me at ease. For example, Día de los Muertos—the Day of the Dead—is an exuberant dance with the ancestors, a chance to welcome those who have passed on from this thread of the universe for a little while. In the absence of such joy, I only knew fear. And I was influenced by the ghosts I saw on TV—gruesome, scary, and meant to harm. What a strange thing it was: To be so close to a culture, of that culture, but to be so removed from the parts of it I needed to feel whole and safe.

When it came time for college, I was ready to leave. I wanted the peace of sleep without spirits, and I was convinced I would find it somewhere far away from El Paso. I was bound for the suburbs of Chicago, a place as different from home as any I could have chosen and one that failed to deliver the escape I had desired.

In this flat, barren land of perpetual winter, I felt completely estranged from who I had been at home. I was unhappy with my chosen major but couldn't be convinced of a new one. I was shy, and I missed the silly, easy intimacies of high school. I abandoned the things I loved the most—singing, writing—because I was simply too afraid to seek them out in a new form. It stripped me to the bone and laid bare the most essential parts of me.

The spirits were gone too, burrowed somewhere dark and warm where I couldn't find them. The people I met didn't even believe in ghosts—real to me as the snow that poured from the sky every October. Not everyone would acknowledge blurriness at the edge of the horizon or notice the shadows in the periphery, I knew, but I hoped some would. It began to feel as though the world I had been so eager to leave behind was also the only world that would ever make sense to me.

So began my two-step dance of walking back my identity and moving into it, a careful and precise act that lasted for four years. I cannot explain why I did it, except that I wanted to please everyone at all times. When people asked where I was from, I said West Texas instead of El Paso because I was ashamed when people hadn't heard of my hometown. When people learned I was Mexican American, I told them I could speak Spanish because I was embarrassed by my laziness in never having learned. Steam filled my gut as I listened to classmates masterfully conjugate their Spanish verbs, knowing I could barely hold a conversation with people in my own family. I felt exposed by my friends who spoke of their Mexican vacations with delight and authority when I had barely ventured across the border that I could see from my parents' backyard. I blanketed myself in half-truths to hide what I thought was deep humiliation but was really a deep unknowing.

In El Paso, I was Mexican American. Everyone was. But here, making sense of myself wasn't so easy. Away from home, I began to feel that I hadn't been steeped in the culture long enough to make me strong with its flavor, but just enough that you couldn't hide the scent. How could I claim to be Mexican American when I couldn't speak proper Spanish? When I celebrated so few of their holidays and traditions? The only things I knew were the ghosts and the food. I didn't miss the ghosts, but I did miss the food—my mother's crispy chicken flautas, doused in freshly made salsa and served with a side of chile con queso. Two years into college, I discovered a pizza place near my apartment that served tacos al pastor if you knew to ask for them, and I went multiple times a week, a small and simple pleasure that grounded me to who I had been before. Chicago is home to more than twice the number of Mexican Americans than El Paso, something I would have realized sooner if I spent any time exploring, searching for, or learning of experiences beyond my own. I was too wrapped up in hiding myself to realize that people who could've helped me find my home surrounded me.

I did join a student group for other Latinx students on campus—there weren't many of us—but I was too self-conscious to talk about my own complicated feelings about belonging in such a community. We were all so different from one another, and I tried to exist as quietly as possible, awed and ashamed by the scope of my ignorance. I was introduced to Puerto Ricans, Peruvians, Cubans. My entire sense of identity was wrapped around the idea of one specific place—El Paso. I was fascinated by students from New York and Chicago and Miami, who seemed so assured about their place in the world. I never spoke about the ghosts, but maybe they would have understood.

That taste of community led me to the literature class that introduced me to the songs of my ancestors in a way the language hadn't. Even though I grew up on the border, I had only once been assigned a book by a Latinx author. For the first time, at the age of nineteen, I was taught the rich canon of books by and about Latinx people, and in these books, I was shocked to discover the ghosts roamed as free in these pages as they did in my reality.

In Juan Rulfo's *Pedro Páramo*, a young man travels to a ghost town in search of his father. An older woman offers him shelter, but the room isn't quite ready for him. "A person needs some warning, and I didn't get word from your mother until just now," she tells him.

"My mother?" he says. "My mother is dead."

"So that was why her voice sounded so weak like it had to travel a long distance to get here. Now I understand."

I was uneasy about the ghosts of this book—both comforted that others saw the world as I did and bereft that this fearsome world existed as I suspected. I left Chicago as confused as I'd found it, but with the knowledge that the world was so much bigger than me and that I was rooted to it in ways I didn't quite understand.

After graduation, I swore off Lake Michigan and its freezing winds for good. I moved to New York into an apartment where everything seemed to be on the verge of breaking. Despite this, I felt for the first time since leaving El Paso that I had found a place where I felt at home. It was a city where there was always something new to discover and where every block seemed to be hiding a haunting—or maybe I only believed that because it was too magical a place to leave behind for anything, even death. I relished the long nights that I spent in quiet reverie as I walked through different neighborhoods and surrounded myself in a vibrant quilt of languages, cuisines, and identities. I felt a little more connected to myself and my culture simply because I was finally brave enough to step outside.

That easiness faded when I walked into my apartment, a place filled with ghosts. When you walked in, you were greeted by a long hallway that stretched twelve feet between the doorway and the main living space. The path to hell, my roommate and I joked, must be haunted. I kept the truth to myself, but the apartment really was haunted by a mischievous young ghost who wouldn't let us out of the bathroom that sat at the very end of the hallway. We blamed it on the steam from the shower, but I knew it wasn't true. I closed my bedroom door anytime I was in it, locking myself in because I was convinced that if I left my door open, he would stand in the doorway and watch me read, or sleep, or put on my makeup. I was terrified by the prospect of catching a glance of him in the mirror as I brushed my hair and feared that his attacks would soon be more than mischievous—they would be evil, terrible, violent. I was, for the first time in years, transported back to my childhood.

At night, after my walks, I would come home to my haunted apartment, burrow inside my room, and hide under my cocoon of blankets, like I had done in childhood. I wanted this ghost gone, yet I feared the void. Who was I without ghosts? They were an essential part of my being. They were the thing that made me feel whole and real and connected in some small way to the place that birthed me and made me who I am. Without language, without place, without food, without family, it felt like my only tether to my culture. But the panic felt just as it had in childhood; I was still as conflicted as ever. After weeks of sleepless nights, I finally succumbed:

"You need to leave."

I knew the ghost left because I felt alone again, a sharp pain I wasn't expecting. My dad's advice never failed me. Our relationship with the dead was a unique and important part of our ancestral ties, and he understood that better than anyone I knew. It was a complicated, imperfect, and messy relationship. It was beautiful, and it was frightening. I could still find many truths about myself in these ghosts and not yet be ready to fully embrace them.

And soon, I would have no choice.

After my mother died, I stayed with my dad for a month. I needed to grieve in peace, to clear out the remains of her life, to be home for more than a few days over the holidays. I had last left it as my parents' house, and now it belonged just to my dad. After many years away from El Paso, I was struck by my unfamiliarity with it. It existed as a dream in my mind, a foggy and ethereal place that wafted away like dust when my plane landed. It was real, solid, and filled with people I loved, both living and dead. It was still a place where magical things happened on ordinary ground, like the dead coming to say goodbye with a knock on the door or ring of the bell.

A few days after my mother's death, I looked out at the mountain behind my father's house and saw a rainbow perched above it, a luminous crown on its barren peak. It rarely rained, and I had never seen a rainbow in that particular spot. I had a realization as clear as the sky after that Texas thunderstorm: There would be a ghost.

I waited. For days, I did not sleep, but she did not come. More sleepless nights came and went, and when I asked my father why she hadn't come to say goodbye, he told me she wouldn't come to me because she knew I was scared. He was right. I was still too scared of seeing her as a ghost, and now I would have to accept the possibility of never seeing her again. I went back to New York. My apartment, no longer haunted, seemed empty without a ghost.

Years later, I found an outlet for my grief in an unexpected place: a community of brujas who welcomed me into their circle. Their perception of ghosts and the afterlife was similar to my own but more refined and developed. In my fear—and fascination—with ghosts, I had acknowledged their existence, I had acknowledged their power to hurt and to harm, but I had not acknowledged their power to heal. Spirits could be beacons of guidance and support. I thought of the narrator of *Pedro Páramo* and his strange journey through a ghost town and how many of those people in between realms had tried to help him discover the truth.

The brujas in the group spoke lovingly of their ancestors, of the relationships they had forged with them over years of dedicated prayer and homage, of the candles they left burning to light tunnels through the underworld and into their rooms. I began leaving presents for my mother: tea candles, a bouquet of her favorite flowers, a turquoise bracelet I found among her belongings, a tiny bottle of tequila.

I began to honor my complicated relationship with the dead in an attempt to find peace in the supernatural. I realized how primal and fundamental my obsession with spirits was. It wasn't just a hobby, but a sacred and important part of my identity—as a person, as an El Pasoan, as a Latina. I looked around at these women with roots in different countries, with the same innate knowledge of the power of the ancestors. I knew that I had, in my hands, the knowledge of unlocking who I was all along. It is a constant process of knowing and unknowing yourself, with the people who have come before you as your guide. Ghosts aren't always scary. In the process of making and remaking yourself, they are there, too—to show you what came before and remind you that you are rooted to the universe in ways you cannot fathom.

As my perspective changed, my fear dissipated, and I realized I had already seen my mother's ghost.

A few years after she died, on her birthday, I was sitting in my living room in New York City, my cheeks sticky with tears. I was too numb to go for a walk, to turn on the TV, to do anything other than sit and feel too much for too long.

A drop. The thing I remember most vividly is the sound, like a ballooned raindrop on a windowpane.

On the arm of my sofa, just beside my hand, was a ladybug. Never before had I ever seen one in my apartment or indoors in New York City at all. I watched in silence, tranquilized by a potent cocktail of emotions. The ladybug sat still for a few minutes—a beat too long—then crawled down the length of my sofa and disappeared.

Years later, I shared the story with one of the brujas. She told me what I had long known to be true: Sometimes, the people we love use animals or bugs as vectors of their spirit for a short time, to visit us or to give us a message. The ladybug, she said, was the sacrifice. I mourned for that tiny lightning bolt of cherry red, that conduit of my mother's spirit, the symbol that has kept me whole and sane since. But I also remembered the words from *Pedro Páramo*, written by a Mexican man who lived and died long before me: "So that was why her voice was so weak like it had to travel a long distance to get here." I thought about my mother's journey from the afterlife and into my living room, and I finally understood how it was all connected.

My mother knew I was too scared to see a ghost, so she gave me a ladybug—a clear, strong signal across worlds. I saw her more than once, in the exact moments I needed to know someone was watching over me, sitting beside me, pushing me forward with love and grace. Seeing her ghost has given me something close to a feeling of belonging to something bigger than myself and greater than any classification. I still hadn't embraced my fear—my fear of the undead, of the things I didn't know about myself, of my discomfort with calling myself Latina, of my ancestors.

Yet, I feel more comfortable with this idea being one part of the wondrous and fantastic network of living and dead spirits that has such a strong history in the people and cultures that I call my own. In that ladybug, I saw everything I needed to know.

The scariest ghost story I've ever heard was one my father told me. Once, he said, he saw a shadow running across the kitchen, through the sitting room, past the living room, and into the bedroom where I lay asleep.

My father asked it to leave, and as he did, it turned around, and he saw that it was unlike any other ghost he had encountered. Where the head should have been, there were instead dozens of moving frames ticking through swiftly, like a movie reel. It was trying to figure out which face to present to the world; it was trying on dozens of different versions of itself. I was frightened to learn of this story—maybe that will never fully go away—but I was comforted, too. My whole life, I've been trying on different versions of myself, haunted by the weight of the expectations of who I'm meant to be.

How strange and wonderful it is, I think now, that the ghosts don't know who they are either. The ghosts are haunted, too.

Paraíso Negro
Kahlil Haywood

....

When people think about a Spanish speaker they don't necessarily rush to think about someone who looks like me. You know, a brown-skinned, kinky-haired man, at least with my hair grown out. They might instantly think of people who look along the lines of Jennifer Lopez, Eva Mendez, Marc Anthony, or Pitbull. Ignorance and the media have a huge part to play in how this narrative has been shaped. However, I never thought that a Black person being fluent in Spanish was abnormal. It was my reality, what I was surrounded by. I come from a Panamanian family on both sides. Panama is a Central American country located right below Costa Rica, and though the native language there is Spanish, a sizable population of the country's inhabitants is Black. Not only were my parents from Panama, but all of my grandparents were as well. I started kindergarten at four years old in Brooklyn, New York, in 1994. It was around that time that I noticed that people were from different places, and have different accents, and all the while our skin tones could be the same.

Latinx cultures are as varied as much as they are the same. What we call patacones in Panama, Dominicans will call tostones, and Haitians bannann. They are all the same dish—fried green plantain. Haitians make griot, and we Panamanians make puerquito. Both dishes feature fried pork. The dynamics and conditions in which we live are very similar from island to island. This ranges from the social dynamics of being Black on our respective lands and the social justice issues that can stem from that to the physical makeup of the homes that we live in or the types of weather that we experience.

I attended a very West Indian school. There weren't any other Panamanians attending at the time. The kids and teachers were *all* Black, except for our computer teacher, Mr. Mike. Brooklyn is such a melting pot of Black culture, and my grammar school epitomized that. The countries that people were from ranged from Dominica to Trinidad, Grenada, and Jamaica. As I got older, I would let kids know that I was Panamanian and spoke Spanish. They would look at me with confusion. A lot of kids had never even heard of Panama before. Imagine a kid my age having to explain to another kid that your family's place of birth isn't imaginary. From the jump, we weren't able to connect on that foundational level. Something was separating me from the other kids. It wasn't a racial thing. I mean, we were all Black. But I was a different type of Black from theirs. My kind of Black didn't have a distinction that was widely recognized in the early '90s. If someone mentioned that they were West Indian, you already knew a bunch of places that you could narrow down their lineage from. What we now know as Afro-Latino or as Afro-Latinx these days simply didn't exist back then.

During certain times of the school year, like Thanksgiving celebration, or international culture day, we would have potlucks. My mother wouldn't always send a dish from Latin culture; a time or two, she made lasagna. But when she decided to take it back to our roots, no one else had dishes like mine. I just knew that when the time came, I would be the only kid in school bringing my proverbial arroz con pollo. It wasn't popular. It wasn't what the other kids were used to eating. What they *were* used to eating was curry chicken and curry goat. They loved macaroni pie, brown stewed oxtail, or brown stewed chicken. Trust me, I could put away some roti my damn self. I loved a beef patty and a ginger beer. I'm from Brooklyn, after all.

Growing up in a Panamanian household meant that I would eat traditional meals, but we also made a lot of the same foods my classmates ate. I was no stranger to oxtail and stew chicken or macaroni and cheese. But my classmates, at that time in their life, had never been exposed to authentic Latin food. That resulted in none of them really sharing in the dishes that I brought. I remember some teachers trying it. I guess that was to be expected, as they were older and had more exposure to cuisine. They tended to enjoy it, which sort of confirmed for me that I wasn't bugging. It was good stuff. These shorties just weren't hip to it yet.

Looking back on it as I write this, maybe I was bothered. I never really addressed it. I grew to be reluctant to ask my mother to make anything because I just didn't want her efforts to be wasted. She would always find out when these events were though, because she stayed so damn well informed. It's a testament to how great she has been as a parent. She was always very engaged, whether I was happy about it or not. I had grown tired of seeing kids share their dishes and everyone "getting it." You know, liking it. They were already familiar with them. The reluctance kids had to try something new just annoyed me. I was fortunate to have been exposed to a lot of good things from an early age.

I was exposed to different cultures through cuisine by going to different street fairs in the city with my mother and my aunts growing up. I experienced different cultures through music as well. I went to a lot of free concerts as a kid. I can still remember my first concert where I saw Marc Anthony (with a ponytail) perform with La India. They were huge around '95–'96. I also have an older cousin who is into the performing arts and music. His name is Guillermo, also known as Pegasus Warning. I was exposed to his artistry as a kid. I've seen him perform a bunch of times growing up and even recently. He's a drummer that you can see perform late nightly with James Corden's band. I never considered myself to be a sheltered kid. I was moving at a slightly different speed in my development which I owe totally to my mother and my family at large. So when it came to my frustration with other kids' closed-mindedness, I sucked it up and moved on.

Traveling was another way that my exposure to different cultures was manifested. As a kid, I traveled many times during the summer. My mother thought it would be a benefit to my development. As an adult now, I'd say that she was spot on. My mother sent me away to see family in other states or countries. My mother would sometimes travel with me, but most times, I traveled alone, especially once I turned eleven. Summers were long, and they were fun. The time was always well spent.

These trips began in 1995. I had my first opportunity to visit Panama for a family reunion. This was also the first time that I would be traveling without my mother and instead with a group of kids that included two of my cousins — Jhanilka and Jahaira. I was perfectly fine traveling with family. That was the easy part. But I still had some angst. I was a total mama's boy as a child. I went everywhere that she went. So until that point, I hadn't spent much time away from her. My mother saw the importance of me traveling, and even though I was excited, I wasn't sure how things were supposed to work, being alone and all. The reality of being away from her didn't sink in initially.

We knew whom we would be staying with in Panama — my cousins' grandparents, who we affectionately called Abuelo and Abuela. I will admit that I actually thought these were their given names as a younger child. I knew I was in for a good time, but the truth was that they weren't traveling with us *to* Panama. We were meeting them once we touched down at the airport. Before we went to our gate at the airport, I bawled, crying like nobody's business, screaming "Mommy!" while on the line for TSA. This was the point where I would say goodbye to my mother and then go along with the group of kids we were traveling with. My mother consoled me for a second and reassured me that everything would be fine. She pointed at the other kids that I was traveling with and how relaxed they seemed. There wasn't anyone else bugging the way that I was. I was pretty hysterical; I thought I looked crazy. Being that I always wanted to present "cool" or relaxed, I calmed down. It wasn't my first time flying, but it was my first time flying without my mother. That simple fear of the unknown is what I think set me off. Maybe it was just emotions that I needed to get out of the way. Once I did, I was completely fine.

When we landed in Panama, we were greeted by Abuelo and Abuela. I was eager to see just how unlike New York this place was. There wasn't much difference from inside the airport, but it definitely felt different once we stepped outside. It was warm, and there was a really nice tropical breeze. We all packed into Abuelo's beige 1988 Nissan Sentra that played Beethoven's "Für Elise" when you put the car in reverse. As we drove away, I looked out the window and saw my first coconut trees, which was pretty cool. Police officers wore beige uniforms. Damn near all of the cars ran on a manual transmission and were stick shifts, including Abuelo's.

We eventually pulled into "Paraíso," and Abuelo exclaimed, "Do you know what 'Paraíso' means?" I said no. He emphatically responded, "It means 'paradise'!" This would be the first of many English to Spanish translation questions that would ensue over the next two months and future trips to Panama that I would eventually make. Abuelo loved to watch *Primer Impacto*. He asked me, "Do you know what that means?" Of course, I'd try to put two and two together, but sometimes I didn't get it. On that occasion, he responded, "Prime impact!" It was a constant learning experience.

Paraíso is the first and main community that I have stayed in during my travels to Panama. It's located in the former Canal Zone. This is where (you guessed it) you lived if you lived near the Panama Canal. Abuelo's house sat on a hill. The house was a long unit split by a wall in the middle. The next-door neighbors' unit was on the other side of that wall. Abuelo's house had a living room, kitchen, backyard, dining room, and three bedrooms. Not to mention he also had his own mango tree and hammock in the back.

Paraíso was a segregated community in its early years. In 1918, the American workers in Panama were moved to Pedro Miguel, a neighboring town. This resulted in Paraíso becoming a "silver" segregated town. The residential neighborhoods at the time were divided into Hamilton Hill, Jamaica Town, and Spanish Town. As construction of the canal began, living and education conditions were vastly different between the whites and the Blacks. Of course, Black people in Panama didn't get the best of the resources available. They didn't have better living quarters or better-maintained schools. They had to drink at separate water fountains from whites, for instance. That's something we knew to be normal during the same period in the United States as well.

The Canal Zone was formally abolished in 1979. That was around the same time that segregation in Paraíso ended. Prior to this, the US presence in Panama was a military presence in which a lot of the better job opportunities existed on the army bases. The military presence existed due to the Panama Canal construction and the abundance of politics and resources utilized to make that project happen. You know Uncle Sam had to get broken off something if they were going to assist in making such a feat come to fruition. So the US wanted some kind of control over the happenings in the country and over the trade. It was a prime opportunity to have some autonomy over a revolutionary structure that connected the Pacific Ocean to the Atlantic Ocean.

It's important to make these distinctions as Panama has these prejudices as part of its history. The same sorts of inequities that Black people suffered during the civil rights movement of the 1960s in the United States, Black Panamanians suffered on their land too. Being a Black Spanish speaker didn't grant you any sort of passes during this time in Panama. So when you fast-forward to present-day imagery of what makes someone Latino or Black, it makes no sense to think that you can't have one without the other.

Even though Abuelo and Abuela resided in Paraíso, they were divorced. So Jahaira and Jhanilka stayed by Abuela most of the time, and I would stay by Abuelo. They lived near each other, so seeing my cousins was an almost daily thing. Abuela's house sat near the water. Abuelo's house was down the street, around the corner, and up the hill.

My first real culture shock came when I realized that the roofs of homes in Paraíso were largely made of galvanized steel. The process of galvanizing involves covering the steel in a zinc gel to help slow down the rusting. The steel plates are then placed at angles on the roof and contain ridges (like the potato chips). They help to drain water when it rains. It also results in loud-ass noise as the water hits the roof during tropical showers. As we say today, if you know, you know.

Once inside Abuelo's house in Paraíso, I got another surprise—there were *lizards* inside his crib! People who live in Panama live with them! Now, these weren't Iguanas but damn it, they were still lizards. It was another reminder that I wasn't in Brooklyn anymore. Hot water was no guarantee. I took many cold showers during my first summer in Panama and learned how our bodies adapt to the temperature of the water. It wasn't that people didn't have boilers in Panama. They did. But it wasn't customary to always keep them on. So to turn the boiler on and have the water be warm enough would take some time. But when it was time to go, it was time to go. So you bit the bullet and took a cold shower.

Abuela didn't drive, so when we stayed with her, we had a different experience when visiting the city. We called that "going to town." When we did, we took Panama's public buses. The city buses that took you into the communities outside of the city and vice versa were what we consider school buses here in the states. The drivers repainted the buses with all kinds of art like graffiti and cartoons. Every bus had a different personality based off of the art painted on them. There weren't buttons to press or bells to ring when you wanted to signal to get off the bus either. Instead of that, you had to yell "Parada!" in order to let the driver know you wanted to get off. Those moments always came with a hint of anxiety because Paraíso was outside of the city. So when the bus headed back to that side of town, it would pick up so many people on the way out that the bus would end up full. Much like how New York City buses would be packed pre-pandemic, the buses in Panama were no different. Now, you're hoping and praying that the driver heard you yell "parada" or else you'll be passing your stop.

While staying by Abuela, to pass the time, we watched— through steel-mesh fences that were allegedly electrically charged—ships pass by with tons of cargo. They were either going to or coming from the canal. I didn't understand how special it was to be seeing that at the time, but we essentially had the Panama Canal in our backyard. We were literally living by it for months during the summertime and had no idea about the rich history that existed on the land we were on. It's something that you could easily take for granted as a kid. In hindsight, people would kill to have had the opportunity to be that close to such a sight. It's still regarded as one of the modern marvels of our time.

My cousins and I made our own fun. There were two kids who lived next door to Abuelo. That was Mr. Brown's house. We would play with them sometimes too. They were Black as well, and they spoke English! That was totally the contrast from the majority of the other kids that we saw around. We weren't fluent in Spanish, so interactions with the Browns brought a sense of normalcy. It made playing games with them a hell of a lot easier. So whether it was hide-and-seek, or tag, or monkey in the middle, having them around made it easier to pass the time on otherwise quiet days.

One day in particular, I remember playing a game with

Jhanilka with the basketball. It was simple as all hell. I think we were just throwing the ball at each other, playing catch. Now in Latin and Caribbean countries, there are usually long drains that run along the sides of roads that lead to the gutter. There were occasions where we played with the basketball, and the ball ended up rolling down the drain and into the gutter. This time around, Abuelo distinctly asked us to make sure that the ball did not go into the gutter. You see, when it did, it would end up stuck in a pipe that was under the street. Well, wouldn't you believe it, a missed catch by me and an unlucky bounce, and that ball went down the damn gutter.

Now we both felt like we were fucked. Who was going to tell Abuelo? I can't remember how he eventually found out. Jhanilka and I were "squeezing our bam bam" with nervousness as we would jokingly say. What was going to be his reaction? How was he going to get the ball out? Well, eventually Abuelo came out and surprisingly didn't give us a tongue lashing at all. He kneeled down, took the cover off of the gutter hole in the street, and went down into this hole to get the ball out! Who knew there was a little ladder type of thing in there to climb down? After seeing all of that, we made sure to just find somewhere to play away from gutters.

This was my first time really outside of a city environment. I was an urban kid who was being exposed to living life in the country. Here, people just picked fruits off of trees and ate them. Coconut trees abounded everywhere. We picked fresh mint leaves to make tea in the morning. We ate mamones (guineps) straight from the trees when we could, and mangos too. Everything was just a lot fresher. The experience was more natural.

I spent that whole summer growing accustomed to a whole new lifestyle. I saw dragonflies and frogs. I actually saw a local whack a frog with a twig and kill it. For some, in the country, that was a way to pass the time. One of my scariest experiences involved a bat. Nowadays, we can't stand bats for public health reasons. Many think that we can thank them for "The Rona." Well, there was no way I was thinking that deeply about bats, I just knew that I wanted no part of them. As we know, bats cannot see when there is light outside or in a specific area. Just being in a country where bats existed as much as they did was an eye-opening experience.

Abuelo had some family over because we were in the middle of celebrating our '95 reunion. At this point, I had probably been in Panama for about three weeks. Our reunions are usually every two years, and they last a full week. Abuelo used to love to leave his door open at all times of the day. He would usually close it at night. Since people were over and he was entertaining, he left it open that night.

It was packed in the house on that evening, and we were having a ton of fun. Seco (Panamanian rum) and Soberanas (Panamanian beer) were being consumed left and right. There was music playing as well. I can still remember the sounds of Miriam Makeba's "Pata Pata" playing. My family loves the hell out of that song, and I can't front, so do I. But back to the bat!

I happened to be sitting near the door, and as luck

would have it, a bat flew into the living room. In that moment, I felt like everything stood still, and the spotlight was on me. I was petrified, as Eddie Murphy would say. I was scarred for life. There was a live bat flying around the living room wildly! What was even more amusing is that I seemed to be the only one who panicked. My guess was that this wasn't the first time the local family there experienced something like that. It was a day in the life, so to speak, for them. It further drove home the fact that I really was living in the country, and it was nothing like what I was used to. It was a stark contrast. These animals *will* come and see you. Anything can damn well happen here, and that was something that I had no experience with up until that point.

Come to think of it, I've had several interesting experiences with animals in Panama. Dogs on Abuelo's block would chase our car every time we drove down the street. He even said one got hit once while doing that behind someone else. There was also a guy that we used to visit who we would rent videos from. That's right, VHS tapes. He was one of Abuelo's friends, and he had a ton of American movies that played in English without subtitles. If you didn't have cable in Panama, there were limited English channels. The tapes brought a sense of normalcy at times. Having no subtitles felt like having a day off. Abuelo's friend also lived across from a lake.

One thing we did when we visited his friend was look to see if there were any alligators in the water. We were told that there were. If we didn't see any swimming, a common thing we enjoyed doing was picking mangos and throwing them into the lake to see if any gators would begin to stir. Many times they did. Their eyes would peer right above the water level. We knew that we got their attention. We usually watched unless we thought that they were getting too close. In that case, we would dip and dip quickly.

Throughout that summer of '95, I grew comfortable in Panama. The majority of Panamanians that I saw there were Black and that familiarity made things feel like home. I came from the States, where a native Spanish speaker wasn't imagined to be Black. In Panama, it was normal. There were a lot of us—like a Black paradise. As a matter of fact, Panama has Indigenous peoples too. The mestizo—people of mixed European and Indigenous ancestry—are responsible for a lot of the folkloric art called "molas" that Panama is widely known for. Aside from Panama's Black population, mestizos make up a huge amount of Panama's population. They, too, are Spanish speakers who you may not expect to speak Spanish based solely on how they look.

It was imperative for my growth in terms of my worldview for me to have learned how to get along with other kids, even with a language barrier. I expanded my palate for food as well. I don't think there was a period of my life where I ate more empanadas. I was eating mamones, and having tortilla for the first time. I had tamarind juice for the first time, and damn, was it sweet. I even begrudgingly got a little more comfortable with nature, out of necessity. But I gained a sense of pride over that summer, as well as a sense of security in who my people were. They were in abundance. I could now attest to this. I could now have the same convictions and pride that I saw a lot of my West Indian counterparts exude.

A common theme that always rang true to me on this trip was that you really couldn't judge the proverbial book by its cover. I came back home after that summer as a different kid. I came back home knowing that there really were so many other people out there just like me. Going forward, I would no longer be surprised to be seen as a rarity, that I wasn't expected to be Latino because I was Black.

I made several trips to Panama in my life. Four trips, to be exact. In '96, I was so much more comfortable with everything involving the travel. We went with another group of kids again, but the crocodile tears were a thing of the past. The culture shock no longer existed, and that helped with enjoying the time spent there even more.

I went back to Panama in 2000. This was my third trip—my first time traveling alone internationally. My other cousin Adriana joined us on this trip too. It was such a stark contrast from my first trip to the country five years prior. That year what I enjoyed most was watching wrestling pay-per-views for free at Abuelo's house. In Panama, the pay-per-views aired on network television. It was a treat because I had no cable back in Brooklyn at the time. By that age, I also graduated to drinking a full bottle of beer with Abuelo rather than the half bottle I was relegated to at six and seven years old.

The older we got, the more we visited El Chorrillo. Chorrillo is another town in Panama that was more urban than Paraíso. Think of it as a Brooklyn circa the 1990s. It was more heavily populated, and there always seemed to be things to get into. My cousin Kyshia stayed there when she visited Panama, and her father still lives there. When we visited them, Jahaira, Jhanilka, Adriana, Kyshia, and I ran free through the streets. We weren't causing any trouble, but we would just be out hanging. When we returned to Chorrillo, we learned that they enacted a curfew where kids couldn't be outside after 9:00 p.m., and so most times, that's what we would abide by.

By this time, I was twelve years old, and on one occasion, we were inside, and it was after 9:00 p.m. We wanted some ice cream. There was a lady a few houses down who sold it in little containers. So Jahaira, Jhanilka, Adriana, and myself, led by Kyshia, game-planned to run to this woman's house at warp speed to buy the ice cream. The goal was to run, knock, get in the house swiftly, purchase, and get back without the police seeing us. It wasn't quite like a summer blockbuster high-speed chase, but it was intense. We succeeded and live to laugh about it today.

With every trip to Panama, I grew more comfortable with my ethnicity. Places like Paraíso and Chorrillo were filled with Black people. Although there was a language barrier, nothing else about me really stood out. You could've taken me for a local. Once I got back home after that trip, I realized that being Black and living in Brooklyn, we weren't granted the same benefit of being recognized for our plethora of ethnicities. A lot of people can't tell the difference between a Scottish person and someone from England, but we know that they have differences culturally.

Even after all of my trips to Panama, and becoming

even more comfortable seeing Black people be the Latin culture there, I was taken aback in the States by people who still acted surprised by a Black person who spoke fluent Spanish. Many of these cases were evident in the food and hospitality industry. Through my many travels with my mother, I witnessed how we were treated when certain people were serving us. Many times, dishwashers and busboys at restaurants are of Latin descent, in New York at least. These folks, their counterparts, and Americans would view them as Spanish "looking" people. There have been countless occasions at eateries and other businesses with my mother where said worker didn't perform a service optimally. Whenever my mother spoke Spanish to the worker, all of a sudden, we were taken care of a lot better. They became best friends on the strength of their commonality of language. It sounds very endearing and hopeful. But I didn't dig the fact that we were treated differently because we weren't seen as "one of them" initially.

This opened my eyes to another shape this type of blindness can take when you aren't seen as Latino. I realized that this was only the beginning. Ultimately, it's a case of being profiled here in the States. We're seen as "Yankees" to other West Indian Islands and Latin countries. In other words, we're seen as Black Americans from the United States who have no knowledge of other cultures. So who would assume *we* spoke Spanish, you know?

When you're in Panama as a Black person, you aren't seen as an outlier when you speak Spanish. It's well-documented these days that there are Black people all over Panama. People are used to it. Now, that's not to say that colorism doesn't exist there, because it does. But that's independent of the understanding that Black people can be fluent in Spanish; that's a normal thing. The only difference that I can see between a Black person in Panama and a Black person in the States is the style of dress. Back then, wearing high socks and soccer jerseys was a regular occurrence in Panama. I saw a lot more sandal wearing out there, which is pretty different from the fashion in NYC during any period of my lifetime. But otherwise, Black people in Panama felt very much like what I had been used to.

We know that it's a very real thing for white people to be able to span lands and cultures. We have the knowledge that white people can speak various languages, and we have never batted an eye. Yet, Black people historically seem to have been made to fit under one umbrella many times. I believe this is the case because, across cultures, Black people suffer more. They are the least considered out of most groups of people, aside from Native Americans. That isn't the case for the white people, so they don't get lumped together. Black people don't get the benefit of the doubt—we get the short ends of the stick.

As I got older and went on to high school, I met more Panamanians. The general population seemed to be a lot more aware of who we were, and attending a larger school raised the likelihood of me meeting more people like myself. While in high school, I encountered another issue as it pertained to addressing my ethnicity. This was a time in life where taking standardized tests was going to become a regular thing. Having to prepare for them was one thing that was annoying. What was also annoying was filling out demographic information. For instance, many times, when filling out these sections, you don't get a choice to merge your race and ethnicity. You'll see labels that read "Black (not of Latin descent)." I always felt that I was both, and very much fully both. What distinction are they really trying to make here? It's confusing to me because if I don't utter the word "hola," you wouldn't even know that I was a person of Latin ethnicity. Having a feeling of limbo in those moments as an Afro-Latino person isn't fair. The process just doesn't feel inclusive enough.

I would be remiss if I didn't mention what ethnicity I have often been comically mistaken for—Haitian. This happened an absurd amount of times, especially in college, since many of my friends are of Haitian descent. I think that I became "Haitian by association" in large part due to that. It was so bad at times that I have been spoken to in Creole without being asked if I spoke the language. It literally was assumed, and I was left looking like a deer in the headlights. I have explained to people that I went to school with tons of times that I am, in fact, Panamanian. I was always jokingly told that I *looked* Haitian. I'd always respond, "Well, what does a Haitian look like?" I always knew this question was hollow because I grew up understanding that people couldn't see my ethnicity. They would almost be sure I was of Caribbean descent.

It's important to bear in mind that there is so much more to people than what meets the eye. I'm privy to feeling this way, probably in large part because of how I grew up. I have a heightened sense of awareness on this issue, and naturally so. I try to take opportunities that I have to impart those perspectives to people when they become available.

I wouldn't return to Panama again until 2014 for yet another family reunion. I was three years out of college and twenty-five years old. This time I returned with the usual suspects of Kyshia, Jahaira, and Jhanilka, as well as our mothers and Jhanilka's husband, Anthony. We stayed in the city. But we also took trips into Panama's rainforest, which I had no clue they even had up until that point. We fed a monkey out there as well as revved the boat's motor to get the apes to respond back to us from deep in the rainforest.

It was fun to experience Panama as an adult. We all got to experience the nightlife, ordering bottle service at their bars for the low. We also got to ride their version of a party bus called "La Chiva Parrandera," which even had a live band on it! The big-time beer brand there now seems to be Presidente and no longer Soberana. There's also a plethora of resorts there, such as Playa Blanca, which had a black sand beach that we were able to experience. Panama has become a lot more developed, so the exposure of Afro-Latinx culture is certainly on the minds of a lot more people.

Things have come a long way. I think a huge part of that has been the advent of the internet and social media. The world is a lot smaller than it was in 1995. We communicate with each other within milliseconds, no matter where we are. With that ability, people have become more knowledgeable about other countries. Travel has become a trendy thing, and I'd say with good reason. Panama has seen a consistent and gradual increase in tourism between 2005 and 2016, according to the Census Center for Economic Studies data. The travel industry has benefited a ton from technological advancements. People are more open to learning about other cultures. When people post pictures of places they visit, it serves as free advertising for the locales. It influences anyone who ends up viewing the post. It increases curiosity and eventually tourism. Once you increase travel and meet all of the people, you have no choice but to have a more varied view of the world. More recently, it isn't an anomaly to see a Black person speaking Spanish fluently. People have a lot more knowledge than they had decades ago.

Seeking change certainly isn't a one-stop-shop sort of mission. It really does take commitment. It's a process. We have to remain deliberate. We will still have to continue to make these distinctions with some folks. But there is a wealth of resources available now that didn't exist years ago. There's the knowledge that can be attained through Google searches that can school you on the nuances of race and ethnicity. This curiosity is important to have when dealing with people and learning about cultures. These are all conduits to furthering race relations in the US as well. The premise of seeing things beyond yourself and your interests would help the human race as a whole. The ability to understand, and the desire to be understanding, are extremely underrated characteristics to have.

Of course, there's still work to be done. People in positions of power across all industries need to be able to recognize us as distinctly as they recognize other ethnicities. Everything from FAFSA forms to job applications should account for the intricacies of the Black diaspora. I should never have to be in a position again where I have to continue asking myself, where exactly should I check off? How Latino am I? How Black am I? Being Afro-Latino, Afro-Latina, and Afro-Latinx should be recognized. I applaud businesses that keep inclusion at the forefront of all of their practices. Inclusion in today's society should be used to inform all decisions. Being inclusive is not only applicable to balance and consideration of race and ethnicity. Inclusion should take into account the sensitivities and opinions of genders, educational levels, and ages.

To progress in a way that is necessary for more people to thrive in this country, the selflessness of decision-makers must be paramount. The change starts at smaller and less pronounced levels. It begins with inclusion. Inclusion informs, inclusion educates. It should bring about the awareness necessary to bring legislation that can provide necessary changes for marginalized people.

To be seen and to be included is no small thing. People have risked their well-being, their lives, and their freedom in the fight for inclusion. No longer living in shadows or living silently is necessary. As a wise man once said, "This thing is bigger than Nino Brown!" We have to continue to challenge the systems in place that stunt our reach. How do we go about making decision-makers see the importance of making these distinctions among Black people? For one, we can't stop speaking about it. We have to continue to educate those who don't know and do so with conviction. I find it interesting that white demographic information usually isn't varied.

Whether we're Black or Afro-Latinx, we know the world sees a Black person in front of them. We live the Black experience just as much as we live the Latin experience. It's something to never be silent about. We span such a vast array of lands. It needs to be understood that people's minds need to be opened just as vastly. I've had the privilege of going back to my family's homeland and seeing firsthand things that so many others haven't had the opportunity to see here in the States. Paraíso is a lot of things. There's beauty in it. It's peaceful—a place where we created a lot of fun. But make no mistake what it really is at its core: Black. It has given me all of the words to express how important it is for us to be recognized. So I will never be silenced. If that wasn't as clear to me in Paraíso, it damn sure is now.

Cuban Impostor Syndrome

Zakiya N. Jamal

Growing up on Long Island, my high school was more diverse than others but still overwhelmingly white, so when a new guy in school mentioned he was Cuban, I couldn't help being excited.

"I'm Cuban too!" I said without hesitation.

Now, I can remember so clearly the look of skepticism on his face and in his voice when he said, *"Really?"* But back then, I either didn't notice or decided to brush it aside.

"Yeah," I told him. "My grandma's from Cuba."

"Okay."

That was it. End of conversation. He turned away from me.

I hadn't been looking for someone who was Cuban or someone I'd have something in common with, but when I found him, I thought it was really cool. For the briefest of moments, I considered telling him about the best Cuban restaurants in the area and asking him if he knew the same music I'd always hear at family parties. I wanted to ask if he pronounced plantains the right way (it's *plan-tins*, not *plantains*). I felt like there was so much for us to discuss, and yet he didn't feel that way at all. Instead, I was dismissed as if my being Cuban was unbelievable, which is almost laugh-able to me now.

The boy was white-passing. He had blond hair and pale skin and, like me, no one would have ever guessed by look-ing at him that he was Cuban. But while I didn't question his ethnicity because of his race, he didn't offer me the same courtesy. The dismissal made me feel like I'd been given a Cuban test and failed.

At the time, my mind didn't automatically go to racism or colorism. Though my grandma is as dark as I am, the members of our family come in all shades, and some are even white-passing, like the boy in my school. Although we looked different, we were all treated the same. I was never made to feel less than or even teased because of what I looked like. We were all Cuban, and we were all equal.

Or at least I thought we were.

After that conversation with the boy in my school, my eyes were opened. I didn't have the words for it yet, but I knew it was my Blackness that cast doubt on my authen-ticity as a Cuban person. I knew that if one of my lighter-skinned cousins had met this boy, he probably wouldn't have dismissed them.

The realization was a slow unraveling in me that led to what I now refer to as my Cuban Impostor Syndrome. Similar to the way I would often feel like I couldn't call myself a writer because I wasn't published, I started to think I couldn't say I was Cuban because I didn't fit the mold of what a Cuban should be.

It started with my race, but then started to spiral. I began comparing myself to the other Latinx people around me.

On my street, there were two other Latinx families. One I didn't know very well, but the other was close friends with my aunt and cousin whose home my mother and I later moved into. The family was Puerto Rican, and while I knew they were not perfect, to me, they were what a Latinx family was supposed to look like.

Though the father was dark like me, the rest of them were light-skinned with curly hair. When their extended family came over, they switched in and out of Spanish with ease, having conversations I could barely follow. Even little things, like their names being Spanish while my name, Zakiya, made people think I was from an African country rather than Cuban, began to fill me with envy and made me feel inauthentic.

Being around my friends at school was no better. My Colombian friend invited me to her quinceañera, and I remember thinking, why didn't my mom ask me if I wanted one? Then I realized it probably never occurred to her that I would want one, and why should it? None of my cousins had quinces, and my mother never had one either, something she hadn't taken issue with since she viewed the ones she'd attended growing up as way too much work.

I had never dreamed of having a big quince, but watching my friend celebrate hers with her family, following in a tradition that her relatives had all participated in, I felt like I had missed something. Why wasn't my family like that? Why did we let go of this tradition that was inherently part of our culture?

Not only did we not do quinces, but we also didn't open our Christmas gifts on Christmas Eve instead of

Christmas Day like other Latinx families I knew did. We also didn't celebrate Three Kings Day and instead celebrated Kwanza. However, the most glaringly obvious difference between the other families I knew and us was that we did not speak Spanish.

Many of my friends didn't speak Spanish fluently, but most of their parents did. That was not the case for us. My grandma didn't teach her five kids Spanish because she wanted them to be fully assimilated into the US. She felt that if they spoke Spanish or even spoke English with an accent like she did, people would look down on them, lessening their opportunities here.

This thought process was one I'd heard from others, and it's a common practice for many immigrants. Still, while it's an understandable fear, especially in a country where non-native English speakers are often yelled at to "Speak English!" it felt like a loss to not know my grandma's first language.

My mother feels similarly and has always resented the fact that her mother never taught her Spanish. For a long time, I remember my mom was determined to get us to learn. She listened to educational Spanish CDs in the car when she'd drive me to and from school, and when I was in elementary school, she put me (along with my cousin) in Spanish lessons in the hope that we'd become fluent. She even convinced me to take a Spanish course when I attended the John Hopkins Center for Talented Youth program in Mexico, saying that it would help me learn the language. To this day, she proudly claims I came back speaking Spanish fluently, but I have no recollection of this.

Whether it was my mother's want for me to be fluent or my own desperation to have this connection to my Cuban identity, I too became invested in learning Spanish. However, by the time I was a senior in high school, I'd been studying Spanish for about six years and still hadn't mastered it. As much as I wanted to be able to speak to my grandma and other family members in their native tongue, the truth was the Spanish they taught in school wasn't my grandma's Spanish. That wasn't something I could be taught in a classroom no matter how hard I tried, and I became so frustrated that I stopped trying.

I think that's a similar story for most of my family. We've all made our own attempts and have varying degrees of understanding when it comes to Spanish, but none of us really know the language the way my grandma does.

Currently, my grandma is living with my mom and me, and I'll hear her on the phone constantly talking rapid-fire Spanish to her cousins and friends. While it makes me smile to hear her excitedly sharing chisme, it hurts me sometimes that I cannot do that with her. What hurts more is the realization that our family's connection to the language stops with her. Even my cousins who speak Spanish learned it from their non-Cuban parents, so it's not really the same.

Like my mom, a part of me does resent my grandma for not sharing the language she loves so much with her children, but I can understand and sympathize with why she did it. Besides wanting what she believed was the best for her children, I suspect she may have also had another reason not to speak Spanish in the home. Her husband, my grandpa, was Jamaican and didn't know any better.

Though my grandma has never said it, I cannot imagine that he would have allowed her to speak to their kids in another language he could not understand.

Regardless of my grandma's reasons, the fact that I didn't grow up in a Spanish-speaking home was another thing to add to my "I'm Not Really Cuban" list.

On a day-to-day basis, I didn't often dwell on this list. Often, I didn't think about it at all. However, in situations like the conversation with that boy in my high school, this feeling of being inadequate would take over, and I'd pull the list back out and be reminded why I was an impostor.

This happened again when I started applying for college scholarships. My mom, a single mother, was adamant that I take advantage of every opportunity and apply to any and all scholarships that pertained to my background. That included applying to the Hispanic Scholarship Foundation. Looking at the website and all the information about the program made me hesitant. I didn't see people on the site who looked like me. The testimonials from former recipients came from people with names like "Rodrigo" and "Marisol." My impostor syndrome flared up, and I knew I would not fit the bill of what they would be looking for.

I couldn't find the words to tell my mom that, though. I worried she'd be mad at me for even thinking that I wouldn't qualify for this scholarship, or worse, she'd see my insecurities reflected back on her. Because if I didn't really feel like I was Cuban, then who else was there to blame except her, my direct connection to my Cuban heritage?

For those reasons, I applied for the scholarship without complaint, and, as I had feared, I didn't get it. Rationally, I knew that thousands of people applied, and there were more people who didn't get a scholarship than who did. Also, because of my application, I was put on the Hispanic Scholarship Fund's email list, and they continued to send me updates about opportunities they offered to help people like me succeed. However, I dismissed all of that. Instead, I added this "loss" to my list of failings and decided when it came to being Latinx and Hispanic, I did not measure up.

This would be something I'd continue to combat for a long time and sometimes still struggle with. Rather than looking at all the things that did make me Cuban, I would always focus on all the reasons why no one would ever suspect I was. It got to the point where I stopped even feeling comfortable saying I was Cuban or Latinx. I didn't want people to question my legitimacy and then be unable to prove myself. For a long time, I was convinced that it was better to keep my Cuban identity to myself rather than try to engage with the Latinx community and be rejected. This was the mindset I had as I prepared to go to college.

When deciding what school to attend, I wasn't looking at the Latinx community of the schools because I didn't feel like I had anything to do with it. My main focus was on the Black community because that was where I felt more comfortable. While my family didn't fit into my ideas of what a perfect Latinx family should be, there was no doubt in my mind that we were Black.

Although my father passed when I was young, my mom would always tell me stories about how "down for the cause" he was. For instance, Jamal wasn't originally his last name; it was Jones. My father apparently didn't want the "white man's name," and so when he was old enough to change it, he chose the Arabic and Swahili name "Jamal," which means handsome.

Similarly, when I came around, my mother didn't want me to have a boring or common name like her own (Sharon), and she gave my older brother permission to pick out a few names from a book of African names my parents had gotten. Hence how I became Zakiya Nailah Jamal.

From a young age, my mom made sure I knew that Black was beautiful and that our culture and history were meant to be celebrated, always. She was intentional in always giving me picture books with Black characters, and I only had dolls that were Black.

Along those same lines, I grew up with a diverse group of friends, but my closest friends were almost all Black. So when I was looking at colleges, the majority of which were predominantly white institutions, or PWIs, I knew I could only go to a school where I'd still see people who looked like me there.

That's why I was so excited to be invited to Georgetown University's Hoya Saxa Weekend. The program was an all-expenses-paid trip to the school specifically for prospective students of color from low-income families. The purpose of the weekend, which coincided with their Georgetown Admissions Ambassador Program (GAAP) for all prospective students, was to allow Black, Indigenous, and People of Color, or BIPOC, the opportunity to see what the school was actually like for minority students. At that point, I was already pretty decided on Georgetown, but I couldn't pass up the free opportunity to really make sure this was the perfect school for me.

Though my focus was on seeing what the Black community looked like at Georgetown before I even arrived on campus, it was the Latinx community I found myself drawn to. Georgetown had booked the students who were coming from New York City or nearby areas like Long Island on the same charter bus. It was there that I met a girl who would become one of my good friends. Unlike me, she was Dominican and proud. Surprising myself, I ended up telling her I was Cuban, and then she surprised me by openly embracing me as a fellow Latinx person. For the next four hours of our bus ride, we bonded, talking about our excitement for the weekend, our families, and more.

Once we arrived on campus, we split ways to be with our prospective student hosts, but throughout the weekend, we continued to run into each other at the program's events. Then one night, she told me about a party happening at La Casita, an on-campus town house that was centered around hosting events for Latinx students as well as being a home and a safe space for them to gather. Out of curiosity, I agreed to check out the party with her and a group of friends we'd made over the course of the weekend.

As soon as we walked into the house, we were enveloped by the smell of tamales, arroz con pollo, and beans coming from the kitchen and the sounds of loud music and laughter rising up from the basement. People we didn't know greeted us as if we were old friends and we were quickly shuffled downstairs to the real party.

The music was loud, but the people were louder, yelling back and forth in English and Spanish as they danced to everything from "Gasolina" to "Suavemente." More visiting students came, and we danced together, attempting to salsa and bachata where there was no room to do so. No one questioned why we were there, and there was no gatekeeping. That night, I embraced the music and dances, and it took me back to memories I'd forgotten.

These songs and dances were the ones I remembered doing with my family at parties. I knew the words to the songs because they were the ones I grew up with, and I knew the foods because I'd had them before. For so long, I had gotten caught up in all the things I wasn't when it came to being Latinx that I had forgotten how much being Latinx and Cuban was inherently a part of me. Maybe my family couldn't speak Spanish or didn't uphold all the traditions, but we had celebrated our culture in other ways. In our own ways.

As I partied with my friends, I stopped worrying about if I was dancing wrong or if I messed up my Spanish while screaming the lyrics to my favorite songs. I fully enjoyed myself because no one treated me any differently than anyone else because no one cared. Everyone was doing their own thing and letting loose in this space where we were free to truly be ourselves without judgment, and I was left with this feeling of belonging that I hadn't felt in a long time. I'd found my community again.

The acceptance I felt at La Casita solidified my decision to go to Georgetown, but when I started school in the fall, I reverted back to my old ways, still feeling too unsure of myself to really engage with the Latinx student groups. So, while I continued to attend parties at La Casita, that was the extent of my involvement in the Latinx community. Instead, I did what I had always set out to do. I focused most of my time on going to events hosted by the Black Student Alliance and at the Black House, a house on campus dedicated to supporting the Black community, similar to La Casita.

As an Afro-Cuban, Black issues are inherently my issues, so I have no regrets about doing that, but I do regret not standing with my fellow Latinx peers when the time came.

My junior year at Georgetown, La Casita was gone. While La Casita and Black House were similar, they were not the same. Unlike the Black House, which was run by the Center for Multicultural Equity and Access (CMEA), La Casita was a house students applied for through the Office of Residential Living each year. I don't know if it was because no one applied for La Casita that year or if the housing office denied their application, but La Casita ceased to exist. Suddenly the place where I found a piece of myself again was gone.

Although I was upset, I didn't do anything about it. I shrugged it off as a loss and moved on. In my mind, there wasn't really anything I could do about it, and I think, for a while at least, many people felt the same way.

However, in my senior year, the university asked

Latinx student leaders on campus to put together the first university-sponsored Latinx Heritage Month program. Various Latinx organizations came together and hosted a number of events throughout the month to celebrate our culture and heritage, including a panel on Latinx identity at Georgetown, which opened a larger conversation. Where was our place on campus? Why didn't we have our own space? How could the university give us this platform for a month and not acknowledge us for the rest of the year?

We wanted a home for ourselves like the Black House, and, moreover, we deserved one. It was not fair that it was up to us to ensure we had our own safe space each year. A home for the Latinx community should be a guarantee, not simply a possibility.

The students who were chosen to plan the Latinx Heritage Month programming became the Latinx Leadership Forum. Through their conversations, the idea for a new home for the Latinx community was born. Soon petitions and protests were calling for action from the university. In the spring semester of my senior year, a proposal was put forward to university administrators for La Casa Latina, which was approved before I graduated. Now, like the Black House, La Casa Latina is run by the CMEA and is ingrained into Georgetown, making it a permanent space for Latinx students to build community.

This was a huge win for us, but I had nothing to do with it. Honestly, I can't even remember if I signed the petition, much less went to a protest. I could make a number of excuses for why I didn't step up, but they all fall flat. The truth was, I convinced myself that someone else could handle it, and my help wasn't needed. I decided this wasn't my fight, even though it was.

I had ostracized myself from the Latinx community because I felt I wasn't welcome in it, but how could I wish to be welcomed into a group that I didn't have the courage to stand up for and support? For that reason, I will always be ashamed for doing nothing when there was so much to do.

With that said, I cannot deny the fact that when I remember this movement, I don't recall anyone leading it who looked like me, nor do I remember any conversations about what would be done to help the Afro-Latinx community. If this was a concern that was brought up in the petitions or protests, it wasn't a big one, and that didn't go unnoticed, especially when there had already been accusations about anti-Blackness amongst the Latinx community at Georgetown.

Though I'd never experienced it myself, I remember one weekend my friends and I were going to a party hosted by a Latinx fraternity on campus. Before we even made it to the door, a group of Black girls told us not to bother.

"They wouldn't let us in," one girl said.

"What do you mean?" I asked. "I thought it was a free party."

The only time I'd ever been denied entry into a party on campus was when I was trying to sneak into a running club party when I was a freshman and didn't know people actually paid dues to run. This idea that someone wouldn't let us into a party that was open to all made no sense to me.

The girl rolled her eyes. "It is, but they won't let us in."

I had the feeling I knew why, but I didn't want to believe it. I'd been to parties like this before, and I was pretty sure I had friends at that party. This girl, who I wasn't all that close to, had to be mistaken. But I asked anyway.

"Why not?"

"They're not letting anyone like *us* in," she said pointedly.

Her words punched me in the gut. Besides the fact that this girl was implying people I probably knew and may have been friends with were racist, it was also a confirmation of all my fears. I was going to be kept out of this party because of what I looked like, even though I was just as Latinx as the people inside. I didn't want to believe it, so rather than confirm what the girl said, my friends and I didn't even attempt to enter the party.

Later, I considered asking around about it. My friend, who I'd met at Hoya Saxa weekend, had also decided to come to Georgetown, and I knew she knew people in the fraternity, even if she hadn't been at the party herself. But the idea of making that accusation of people she was potentially closer to than she was to me terrified me. Would she be offended that I would suggest such a thing or, worse, would I end up finding out something I didn't want to know?

Ultimately, I decided to let it go. I convinced myself that, whatever happened that night, the people blocking entry into the party weren't my friend or anyone I knew. It was the hosts of the party, and my friend probably didn't even know Black people were being turned away. She was blameless.

It was easier to believe that was true than to actually

find out for sure. Still, as much as I wanted to avoid a conversation about anti-Blackness, it was unavoidable, especially when discussions about being Afro-Latinx began rising up on campus.

At the time, the term Afro-Latinx was new to me. I was highly aware that I was both Cuban and Black, but in my mind, these two things were separate. When I listed my identities, I'd say I was Jamaican and Cuban on my mom's side and African American on my dad's side. Without thinking about it, I associated my Blackness with my father, the African American part of me, not understanding the African diaspora.

As I was making these discoveries for myself, many of my fellow classmates were doing the same. However, as more and more people began referring to themselves as Afro-Latinx, some Black students were skeptical.

"Why every Latinx person out here trying to claim they're Afro-Latinx just because their lips are a little big?" one of my friends tweeted. "Y'all just want to use the n-word."

It was a sentiment I'd heard before and one that certainly existed at Georgetown. A group of light-skinned Afro-Latinx people would come into an event at the Black House, and there would be side-eyes and raised eyebrows. Some Black students felt like their space was being encroached on, and the skepticism was clear.

My Hoya Saxa weekend friend began to identify as Afro-Dominican, and as a light-skinned person, she was one of those people who caught side-eyes from Black students.

"Why do I have to prove to people that I'm Afro-Latinx?"

she once asked me. "Look at my features—you can tell I'm not white. My sister is literally a shade lighter than you. It's ridiculous."

The role reversal was not lost on me. For the first time, she felt what I often felt when we walked into Latinx spaces together. While people would welcome her with open arms, there was always a hesitation with me, this question of, "Is she Latinx too, or is she just trying to hang with us?" My friend wanted to be accepted into the Black community the same way I desperately wanted to be accepted into the Latinx community, and it was frustrating for both of us, but it wasn't exactly the same.

Although I understood where my friend was coming from, it wasn't hard for me to understand why Black students wanted to keep their space separated from people they weren't sure they could trust. Anti-Blackness has always existed in the Latinx community. There are the people who are out-and-out racist, but there are subtler things, too. I've heard people worry about getting "too dark" or "too brown," as if being dark-skinned is automatically undesirable. I've never seen my grandma's natural hair, only knowing the relaxed then curled style she's worn my entire life.

On top of that, we've seen Latinx celebrities like Camilla Cabello and Gina Rodriguez be called out again and again for using the n-word or making racist and discriminatory comments. We've watched videos of Latinx police officers involved in the killing of Black people and then had to listen to too many people in our community come to their defense.

The truth is, the Latinx community has a lot of work

to do to course correct the racism and colorism that has plagued us for years, and Afro-Latinx people need to remember that this term was made to combat anti-Blackness, not to give people a ticket into Black spaces. Yes, it is unfair that some Afro-Latinx people may feel unwelcome at Black events, but if you've been passing as a non-Black Latinx person, then you have to recognize your privilege. Our experiences are not the same, and there is a big difference between your authenticity being questioned and Black people being barred from a party because of the color of our skin.

Being Afro-Latinx is complicated. The term is supposed to acknowledge that people can be of African descent and also Latinx, but often these two halves of ourselves are at war, both externally in the way our two communities engage with each other and internally in the ways we choose to present ourselves. While it's up to the community as a whole to make sure Afro-Latinx people are acknowledged and accepted, it was up to me to start acknowledging and celebrating the Cuban part of me again.

I took my first steps forward during my commencement week at Georgetown. During the week, CMEA hosted three multicultural graduations: Asian Heritage for Asian American and Pacific Islander graduates, Harambee for anyone in the African diaspora, and Despedida for the Latinx community. It was at these ceremonies that students received their multicultural stoles to wear during the larger commencement ceremony for all students.

It was a given that I would attend Harambee, but I found myself unsure about whether or not I should do Despedida. I wanted to attend and wear the stole that would mark me as Latinx at graduation, but my imposter syndrome crept in. I worried I'd have to prove I deserved my stole in some way and that I'd come up short. Part of me knew this was ridiculous, but the paranoia was still there.

My mother and grandma were both coming down to DC from New York to spend the entirety of the commencement week with me, and that included attending the multicultural ceremonies. All the ceremonies happened on the same day back-to-back so students and their families could attend more than one if they needed to, followed by a reception for all groups.

I couldn't imagine having to explain to my mom and grandma that I didn't sign up for Despedida because I thought some arbitrary person wouldn't believe I was Cuban. I knew they'd be mad and disappointed that not only did I feel I somehow wasn't good enough, but I let those feelings stop them from attending another ceremony that was meant to celebrate all my hard work. Thinking about their reactions made me realize how stupid I was being.

I saw a tweet once that said something like, "Whenever you think someone doesn't like you or thinks poorly of you, ask yourself, did you ever hear them say that? If the answer is no, then recognize you were the one who put those words into your head." That's what I had done. I saw the sign-ups for Despedida. There were no tests or any kind of questionnaire to fill out. All they wanted was my name for when they called me up to the stage. The only person who was keeping my family and me out of that ceremony was me. I deserved to be a part of Despedida and get my stole. My family deserved to see me walk across the stage at graduation wearing it.

So, I signed up, and it was one of the best decisions I've ever made.

During the ceremony, which was in both English and Spanish, the presenters called us up one by one and said all of our names right (even mine). I sat with my friends, and we all yelled and cheered for each other as we went up to get our stoles. It was only my mom and my grandma there for me, but they were loud, and I could hear them as I crossed the stage. Together, we got to be proud of our accomplishments and hear from people within our own community, not the old white guy who was our commencement speaker during the actual graduation later that week.

Then, at the reception for all the ceremonies, there were plantains, rice and peas, egg rolls, mac and cheese, and more. Our professors and mentors from the CMEA and other organizations were there to celebrate us, meet our families, and take pictures. My friends and I laughed, drank, and ate, careful not to mess up the stoles we refused to take off the whole night.

It was clear, from the ceremonies to the reception, that this event was made for us by us, and it was one of my most memorable moments during my entire Georgetown experience.

After this event, I began to really tamp down my insecurities and stand more proudly in the fact that I am Afro-Cuban. That isn't to say I started repping my Cuban flag all day every day, but I did become more confident in speaking about my experiences as a Latinx person.

Since graduating from Georgetown, I've had more and more conversations with my friends and family about being Afro-Latinx, what that means, and how things need to change. The more comfortable I became having these discussions, the easier it was to talk about it in all spaces I occupied, including my professional ones.

Shortly after graduating from Georgetown, I got an editorial fellowship at BuzzFeed, and one of the first things my manager asked us fellows to do was make a list of our identities. What made us who we were? I wrote a lot of things on that list before I finally wrote Cuban. My manager then told me to think about ways I could write about my experience being Cuban, and that led to one of my first posts, "21 Struggles All Afro-Latinos Know To Be True."

The post didn't get as many hits as some of my others did, but I was incredibly proud of it. So many people left comments saying how relatable it was, and to this day, I still sometimes get tagged on Twitter by people who share the post.

After the post went up, the person who managed the Latinx channel on BuzzFeed's Slack messaged me and asked if I wanted to join. Even though it was a small thing (the channel was public; I could've joined at any time), the fact that she personally asked me to join made me feel welcomed into the fold.

In the group, we talked about everything from crowdsourcing posts we were thinking about doing to discussing current events and the culture at BuzzFeed. People switched in and out of Spanish in the chat, but for those of us who weren't fluent, it felt okay to ask for clarification. I never felt excluded, only accepted, and while I didn't need their acceptance, I realized I needed their camaraderie.

As I discovered in college, being open and honest about my background was how I found my people. When I told people I was Cuban, and it turned out they were also Latinx, or better yet also Cuban, we formed a bond. We, at least on some level, understood each other.

This didn't always happen. I've met people who are quick to correct my Spanish in a way that feels more condescending than helpful or who give me that same disbelieving *"Really?"* when I say I'm Cuban, like that guy in high school did. And sometimes, I still have my own internal insecurities about whether or not it is my place to speak up on issues affecting our communities or second-guess myself when giving my opinion on any Latinx discourse. Even in the process of writing this essay, I wondered multiple times if someone else would've been better suited to write about their Latinx experience.

However, whenever I or anyone else makes me feel like a fraud, I remember that it is not my skin tone, my fluency in Spanish, or my name that makes me Cuban. I am Cuban because my mother is, my grandma is, and her mother was. Moreover, I am Afro-Cuban. I am proud to be both Black and Cuban, proud of the resilience that got all sides of my family from the African continent to Cuba, Jamaica, and the US, and proud of our shared history.

It is that pride that I cling to whenever my imposter syndrome attempts to knock me down because as long as I know where I come from, I know exactly who I am.

More Than Nervios
Lilliam Rivera

....

How many will I need?

It's hard to concentrate, to read the labels on the count-less bottles of pills in the medicine cabinet. I'm afraid nothing will be strong enough. I try to make the calcula-tions to figure out how many to swallow. The numbness I've felt for weeks I can no longer shrug off. This situation isn't new to me, I've been here countless times before, but this time I can't hide behind a mask of fakeness. The pain feels never-ending, darkness blanketing everything I see and touch.

How many will I need?

I'm eighteen years old and the first to leave home for college—the first of five kids from a large Puerto Rican family to even graduate from high school. The first to break out, and this is no small feat. However, I don't talk to my parents about how hard it is to attend this state uni-versity. I've never even heard of Binghamton, New York, but I figured four hours away from my Bronx home would be enough for a new start, more space from the crowded apartment in the housing projects we live in. I never men-tion the loneliness I feel on campus or how the weight of solitude is crushing me. I never speak of how I barely have any money, that sometimes I dig into the crevices of the sofa in the hopes of finding change to buy a candy bar for dinner. I never burden them with any of this. I keep it all to myself.

There are not enough pills, are there?

The off-campus apartment I share with my friend Sylvia is empty. Although Sylvia is my best friend, it's hard to convey to her how bad off I am because she's dealing with her own college struggles. She's Puerto Rican, like me, so we speak the same language of hardship, but there are lamentations I'm too embarrassed to voice to the world. Confessions even to a good friend seem too burdensome to share. Whenever she asks me how I am doing, I lie and say I'm okay.

I go to the kitchen to find alcohol, but the bottles are empty. Drinking used to work for me, it was able to numb me enough until I blacked out, but it no longer works. I need something stronger.

The walls in the apartment appear to tilt forward. A chorus of negative voices continues to repeat the relentless tape running in my head since I was a little kid. This time the choir is seductive and clear: I am nothing, and there is no point in any of it.

I keep searching for how to comply, to finally end this chapter of pain.

Depression is a word never uttered in my family. It simply doesn't exist. There are only episodic situations that occur to certain family members. A person may burst out emotionally or violently, maybe during a family gathering, but those who are witnesses to this occurrence accept it as part of the social fabric. It happens all the time. When a loved one suffers any kind of emotional break, whether the person lives here in the states or on the island of Puerto Rico, my family has an excuse to quell any hard questions. Here are just a couple of them:

"El es demasiado serio."

"Ella sufre de nervios."

"No puede aguantar la bebida."

"Tiene que buscarle a Dios."

There is a picture of me taken with my brother and sister when I was about four years old. In the picture, my sister and brother are both beaming with joy. You can see their brilliant light. Then there is me. I am in the middle of the photo with the most serious face. And that became my label. The quiet one. But what if this was a sign of something else, proof of more than just a four-year-old's solemn expression?

My childhood consists of snapshots I barely remember. The few images I do recall are enough: Sleeping in all day—continuous bouts of crying. Never wanting to leave the apartment. In each of these instances, I was expected to snap out of it. I was allowed to indulge in these dark dips only because I was sometimes overlooked. My mother was taking care of five kids. She didn't have time for the much too sensitive, silent daughter.

A negative tape continuously ran through my head, stating I was too ugly, too stupid, and too poor. If I looked around, the evidence was overwhelming. We lived in the projects in the South Bronx. I grew up during the emergence of hip-hop and the crack epidemic. My father ruled our house with a strong and cold hand. I retreated inside myself, where my solitude not only became my sanctuary, it also became my crutch. I created a fantasy world where the aim was always to escape the crowdedness of my home. I preferred a dream state to reality. The only solace I could find was in the pages of my journal and the many books I hid behind, like C. S. Lewis's *The Lion, the Witch and the Wardrobe* and S. E. Hinton's *The Outsiders.* But it was never enough.

Throughout the years, I thought of my tío Ramon, a cop who took his own life before the age of forty. His ghost lingers. He was, and is, dearly loved, but the cause of his struggle is never mentioned nor how he passed away. No one ever talks about it, and to ask would be a sign of disrespect. Hints were given from time to time. Marital problems. Rumors that shift blame to his wife. The lesson I was repeatedly taught was how women were at fault somehow. No one ever spoke of the burden of being a cop and what that could do to a man's psyche. My uncle's presence looms large over gatherings like a big question mark, leaving me wondering if his deep sadness was contagious. If his suffering was a family trait passed down from generation to generation.

To admit to any type of desolation means having to confess such a thing to a doctor. The doctors I always saw as a kid were white. And because my parents always complied with what all medical authorities said, admitting their child might have a problem would also have meant more appointments, terminology they didn't understand, and expensive medication. Depression is a luxury only afforded to people with wealth. This belief is confirmed by the countless scenes presented on my television screen of young white people speaking to a therapist. The requisite lying down on a chaise longue and extolling fears so freely seems like such an anomaly to me. Esos son los blanquitos. It's how they deal with things. Seeking medical help for anything dwelling in the mind is really meant only for a privileged few.

Raised in a family of strict Catholics, my parents instilled in me the idea of a strong God who hears your prayers if you humble yourself enough. The sentiment was an honest one, but instead of seeing my religion as a strength to uplift me, it became a burden. I started to connect my depressive episodes to punishment for something I did. My God became a vengeful God instead of a loving one. When I turned to religion to find answers, I was given more work. My priest insisted I recite prayers and the rosary daily. He backed up exactly what my parents had been telling me all along, how I needed to pray harder. And I did, but I also learned to hide what I felt. The mission shifted from searching for help to concealing my suffering. My smiles became the mask I showed my family and friends. I leaned into it, but all the while the negative voices continue to roll out their tired script reminding me of how little I was worth.

The shame I felt compounded as I grew older. Secrecy became a way to survive. It is not to say my whole childhood was filled with only gloom. It wasn't. There was absolute joy, too, like when my brothers and I played kick the can outside or when I was taught to dance salsa by my aunts and uncles. But I became very savvy in pushing down my hurt and numbing whatever pain I felt with alcohol. At my first college party, I became so drunk I blacked out and was carried to my room. I don't remember anything. After that, I spent so many hours trying to calculate the right amount of alcohol I can imbibe without being completely inebriated. Like everyone, I experimented with a lot of different things, but most of my experimentation relied on desensitizing, on placing a cloak over my dark thoughts. If I can laugh off moments as a drunk, then no one can really question why I kept placing myself in self-destructive situations. I surrounded myself with people who seemed to be doing the same thing, light friendships concerned only with partying. But the suicidal thoughts increased to the point where I found myself alone in my college apartment counting pills and unable to see any exits.

This low point at eighteen is when I realized how far I was willing to go to stop the pain. A friend intervened that fateful day to keep me from following through with my plan. I even spoke to a counselor. I wish I could say everything turned for me at this point, but it didn't. I went back to my classes and continued to drink, although in moderation. My suicide attempt became a shameful period in my life I buried for years, never once talking or writing about it—until now. But this dark period in college reared its head again years later when the signs could no longer be ignored.

After I had my first child, I suffered from postpartum depression. The week after I gave birth, a close friend called me to wish me thanks, and I responded by saying, "This is the worst thing to have happened to me." She didn't know how to react, so she laughed, but I was serious. I reverted right back to what I used to do as a child, as a nineteen-year-old college student. I never wanted to leave the house. It felt as if I was walking in a complete fog. People who loved me couldn't find a way in. I was far too deep in my depression. Here I was supposed to be celebrating the arrival of a new child, and all I could think was how much I wanted to hide.

Nothing felt safe. I had a great sense of time running out for me. I felt as if I was eighteen again, trapped in an apartment, unable to see a way out. When my thoughts turned violent toward my baby, it was the blaring alarm I could no longer ignore. The hardest thing a person can do is ask for help. Just the act of doing so filled me with such dread I could barely breathe. Admitting I could no longer handle my life meant I failed. My parents taught me to keep moving forward, and being unable to do so was my fault. Those around me could no longer allow me to stay in this state. It was inevitable. I was going to hurt myself or someone I loved. The negative tide in my head was just too strong, and it was trying to take me down. I finally searched for a therapist. It took visiting three different female doctors for me to feel safe enough to speak openly. Even back then, it was almost impossible to find a Latinx therapist, but the doctor I finally met with was a woman of color. With each weekly appointment, the dark clouds slowly lifted.

According to the American Association of Suicidology, Latinas have had the highest rates of depressive symptoms and suicide rates in more than thirty years, but only one in eleven Latinas ever seek treatment. America is built on the belief that if you are a modern woman and you work hard enough, you can have it all. You can have the kids, the job, the family and still have time for daily yoga. This is a myth. No one can do this life alone. Being a woman of color means the obstacles placed in our way are tenfold. When these expressions are being sold, it is usually a privileged woman who is selling them. There is a serious fear of suffering repercussions when you divulge the ugliness inside you to another person. We try to maintain appearances in spite of our deteriorating mental health.

The stigma surrounding mental health therapy is one that is literally killing us. There is a reason why it costs money to seek help. There is a reason why social services are not available to those who need it the most. Our society is beholden to capitalism, and it leaves no room for self-care except for those who can afford it. And I bought into this myth absolutely. If I stuck to the work, then I could ignore what was presently destroying me. I couldn't show any cracks because doing so meant failure. The mask I wore hid the messiness in my head easily until it seeped through the sides and I could no longer contain it.

My current mental health challenges include low-level depression with bouts of anxiety. For the past two years, I've been in therapy incorporating tools to help manage the anxiety, made all the more intense by the pandemic. It's the first time I realize how my mental health is so tied to the physical. How it manifests at night when I'm unable to sleep and how I grind my teeth so hard that I am cracking them one by one. I'm trying all types of things to help offset this. Flash therapy. EMDR. Reiki. Physical therapy. Cognitive therapy. I'm no longer looking for only one solution to help me.

This mental health mixtape also includes prayers. I'm not a practicing Catholic anymore, but my spiritual practice continues to grow. I recently watched the Walter Mercado documentary, *Mucho Mucho Amor,* and I loved this one quote he said, "Nadie tiene a Dios por el rabo." No one has a tie on God. Like Mercado, my religion is a hybrid of my own making. I take it with me everywhere, and I try really hard to listen to my body. No one person has the right medication for me. I don't profess to know the answers. I try different things, most of them free to use. Meditation. AA meetings. Sobriety. Eating healthy. Exercise. There are days when I do none of these things. When I don't check in with my friends. When I stay in bed and cry.

My two daughters are very aware of these bouts. The conversations we've had around self-care are ongoing where I level certain words that make sense to a teenager and again for a young child. They understand when I say I am filled with anxiety, and all I do is cry when I have to force myself to go outside. What does this look like for them to see their mother be so open with her mental health struggles? I only hope the cycle to present pain as weakness ends with me.

As for my parents, they are also learning different vocabulary from their now adult sons and daughters. We explain to them the meaning of the word *depression*. I explain to them why I'm unable to speak to them because of my lows. *Depression* is not a word I'm ashamed of; neither is *therapy.* My parents have never been ones to express how much they love us. It wasn't something they were taught to do. But now, when we speak on the phone, I end the conversation with an "I love you." I want them to see how I am trying to save myself. Self-love is no longer a luxury meant only for a privileged few. I am trying to save my life every day. I value it too much not to try.

How many?

I line up the pills on the dining room table—the glass of water positioned right beside the pills. I take the pills one by one, not thinking through the future and how it will affect those who love me, those who will miss me. I don't play through tomorrow because anguish clouds my vision.

It doesn't take long before I rush to the bathroom, throwing up the pills. For whatever reason, my body rejects them. The pills aren't meant for me, and my future self will forever be grateful.

The phone rings and on the other line is my best friend, Sylvia. She hears right away from the tone of my voice. Something isn't right.

"I can't keep doing this," I say. "I'm sorry."

"I need you to get out of the house right now," Sylvia says. "Hang up this phone and go outside. I'm going to meet you. Go."

Although my actions feel very robotic, as if my body is no longer part of me, I leave the suffocating apartment. For once, I listen to a loving voice, a voice that only wants me to be.

Somehow my legs take me to where Sylvia told me to

meet her on campus. We find a secluded place where we can talk freely, away from any onlookers. I confess my fears, and she doesn't judge me. Sylvia asks me to seek help. I call the college mental health services and make an appointment to speak to someone.

A first step toward changing the trajectory of my life.

A seed planted.

The names of people in this essay have been changed to protect their privacy.

Alaiyo

Jasminne Mendez

"One for whom bread—food—is not enough."
—Lorraine Hansberry, *A Raisin in the Sun*

Prologue

"Damn my eggs! Damn all the eggs that ever was!" My brother stood up and slammed his hand down. A plate of eggs flew off the dining table on stage. Goosebumps scattered across my arms and neck. My hands squeezed the armrest. Ben, my older brother, was becoming a star right in front of my eyes. It was the closing night of the high school fall play, *A Raisin in the Sun,* and Ben was playing Walter—the lead role.

On stage, Ben was a giant. The spotlight followed him from stage right to stage left. His voice filled the room, and when he shouted, it echoed like a loud crack of thunder. The audience held their breath when he spoke. I had never admired or envied my brother more than I did that night.

Ben was a sophomore at the time, and Lorraine Hansberry's *A Raisin in the Sun* was the first time he'd been cast as the lead. I had seen Ben play minor characters in other performances, but this was the first time I felt starstruck by his talent. It didn't matter how many times I sat in the audience and watched the play (three times and counting): the moment he screamed and brushed the plate of eggs off the table always made my heart clench like a fist.

Ben was not a yeller in real life. He never showed this kind of rage. To see him embody a character in this way made me shiver with excitement and a little fear. I didn't know Ben was capable of raising his voice or becoming violent in any way. In fact, I always saw him as the opposite—as a pushover.

Although I was two years younger than him, I was always bossing him around. Actually, as I was my father's daughter, I was always bossing everyone around. But Ben was the one person I knew who would always listen and follow along. If I told him to help me with something, he willingly obliged, head down, without a fuss. Those nights, on that stage, though, Ben was no longer my docile big brother. He was, without a doubt, the stubborn tragic hero of Hansberry's play. In his body, in his voice, and perhaps somewhere even deep inside himself, he became Walter Lee Younger.

As I watched Ben dazzle us with his portrayal of Walter, all I wanted was to learn how to become an actress as captivating as Ben. I wanted to use my voice and body to make an audience forget who I really was. I wanted, more than anything, to become someone other than me.

Growing up, everyone had always made me feel different, and not in a good way. As a military brat, I was used to moving around and changing schools every three or four years. So far we had lived in Alabama, Louisiana, Germany, and now Tennessee, and it was always the same. I always stood out for being the new "mixed girl with the good hair who speaks Spanish." Since elementary school, my teachers would gasp when Spanish rolled off my tongue like water during parent-teacher conferences that I was forced to translate. My classmates used to pressure me to "say something in Spanish" during lunch or recess as if I were some circus sideshow. There weren't many Dominicans living in any of the places we ever lived, and I had no connection to or understanding of what it meant to be a Black Dominican. My Black friends always said I wasn't Black or at least not "Black enough," and to me, Black meant African American. And everyone in my family, including Mami and Papi, always made it clear that we were not African American. We were Dominican, and those were two very different things.

By the time we moved to Tennessee and I started middle school, the isolation and confusion I felt around my identity only seemed to get worse. I would have done almost anything to fit in and be liked because I just wanted to feel less alone. I wanted to be someone the world could love and understand. I wanted to be seen. But I also wanted to be someone less Dominican, less different, less Latina, less Black. I wanted to be enough. Once I saw how much attention Ben received after his performance, I decided theater was the only way.

Act I

Time: 8th Grade
Place: Clarksville, Tennessee
Character: Rosa Parks

My first real spotlight came in the spring of my eighth-grade year. At the beginning of each day after the Pledge of Allegiance, Assistant Principal Mrs. Jones would sigh into the microphone and make hurried announcements over the speakers. One morning in January, while plopping my two-ton US history book onto my desk, Mrs. Jones's zombie-like voice caught my attention.

"Students, our drama teacher, Mr. Cunningham, is seeking performers for the Black History Month Celebration in February. If you are interested, we invite you to join Mr. Cunningham in his classroom after school this Thursday to learn more. Make it a great day or not—the choice is yours. Kenwood Knights forever. Hoorah. Hoorah."

It was only Monday, but I already wanted it to be Thursday. I kept remembering Ben's performance in *A Raisin in the Sun.* I remembered the explosive applause that shook the auditorium when he took a bow. And I could still feel the heat of the stage lights on my skin from where I sat close to the front. I wanted to feel that post-performance rush again, and the Black History Month Celebration was my chance.

Although auditions weren't required, I was determined to show Mr. Cunningham what I could do. Monday after school, I rushed into Ben's room.

"Listen, you have to give me some pointers on acting and performance. I'm trying out for the Black History Month performance."

Ben peered over his thick Coke bottle glasses and smiled. "Cool. What do you want to know?"

"How do I make sure my voice is loud, or like what

should I do with my hands and my body? Do I just stand there or move or what?"

"OK, slow down, slow down. One thing at a time." Ben got up from the bed and stood in front of me. "Stand like someone is pulling a string from the top of your head. Relax your knees and keep your hands still. Take a few deep breaths. From here. This is your diaphragm and one of the actor's most important tools." Ben placed his hand under my breast bone. "Imagine you're filling up a balloon, right here in your diaphragm. Your breath control is always first. If you can control your breath, you can control your voice, your emotions, your character. The core of everything is the breath."

I did as I was told. I felt my shoulders relax, and my feet ground into the floor beneath me. For once, it was Ben who was telling me what to do, and I actually really liked it.

When Thursday rolled around, I practically skipped to Mr. Cunningham's classroom. My hands were sweaty, and my heart thumped like a conga during a fast merengue.

Mr. Cunningham was one of three Black teachers at Kenwood Middle School. He was bald with deep bronze skin and blue-rimmed glasses. He had a thin goatee and a small round belly that rubbed against his belt buckle when he walked. Though I'd never had him as a teacher, I had seen Mr. Cunningham in the halls almost every day, and he always smiled at me and said hello. His energy and joy were contagious. No matter the time of day, he strutted through the halls, swishing his hips and bopping his head as if there was an upbeat pop song playing on loop somewhere in his mind.

Mr. Cunningham started the meeting by explaining that the Black History Month celebration would consist of three Negro spirituals, one modern dance number, and a series of short monologues. He said not everyone would have to perform a monologue, but everyone would have to sing the songs and be a part of the group dance.

"If you are not comfortable singing or dancing," Mr. Cunningham said, wiping his glasses with a purple handkerchief, "then I suggest you leave now." He slipped his glasses back on and waited for a moment. I looked around the room. A couple of students rustled nervously in their seats, but no one got up to leave.

"Excellent! So, before we get to the singing and dancing, who's interested in performing a monologue?"

My hand and three others' shot up like bolts of lightning.

"Great. You all come over here and take a look at the monologues on this table. Decide which one you wanna do and be sure you wanna do it, cause there's no changing your mind once you pick it!"

I rushed to the table at the front of the room. Me and three other students began to grab the neatly organized sheets of paper. Each monologue had the face of a famous African American and a short biography. After a few minutes of shuffling through the monologues and feeling uncertain, Mr. Cunningham walked up and stood next to me. He smiled and reorganized the mess of papers we had made.

"Hi, beautiful. Tell me your name again?"

"I'm Jasminne."

"Jasminne. Yes, that's right. I'm so glad you came today. Have I ever told you that I love your curls? They're absolutely beautiful." He gently patted one of the curls on my back and shook his head as if amazed by what my hair could do.

I could feel my face getting hot. Most people made fun of my curls, saying my hair was too big and too wild and didn't I know about relaxers and a hot comb. It was embarrassing to have a teacher notice and comment on the one part of me I always hated the most. I changed the subject.

"Thanks. Um, can you help me choose something? I'm not sure what monologue I want to do."

"Of course!" He looked me up and down and then pointed. "I think you should try this one or this one." He showed me two different monologues. One was in the voice of Wilma Rudolph, the Olympic gold medalist and track star born and raised in Clarksville, Tennessee. We had learned about her every year in our social studies classes and even visited the museum they had built in her honor near her grave site. Wilma Rudolph was Clarksville's only real claim to fame.

The other monologue was in the voice of Rosa Parks. Almost every year since I started school, I had learned about Rosa Parks during Black History Month. Both Rosa Parks and I had been born in Alabama. Both she and I believed in fighting for what was right. We both wanted to be seen and heard. Her strength had always inspired me. As I read her monologue, I knew that I wanted to be her.

"This one. I want to do this one." I handed Mr. Cunningham the monologue. He seemed surprised. His lips quivered a little as he smiled at me.

"Well, alright, if you think you can play *the* Rosa Parks, then so do I."

For the next three weeks, I memorized, rehearsed, and learned my part. When Ben wasn't busy with homework or learning lines for his own upcoming show, he quizzed me on mine. I recited my lines in the halls between classes. I recited my lines in the shower, on the school bus, before bed, and anytime I was alone. I learned all I could about Rosa Parks and was determined to be the best Rosa Parks anyone had ever seen.

Mami and Papi were excited about my performance because they enjoyed any opportunity to brag about their children. Even though Papi always insisted theater was a great "hobby" and not to be considered for a "real career," he and Mami never missed any of our performances. Mami was so thrilled for me she even helped me put together my costume. I showed her a picture of Rosa Parks, and she helped me find a pink dress in her closet that looked similar. She let me borrow some of her costume jewelry and bought me nude pantyhose and a slip to wear underneath.

Mr. Cunningham had arranged for us to perform at a nursing home before the in-school performance, telling us it would be good practice because these audience members were always kind and welcoming. When we arrived at Clarksville Skilled Nursing and Rehabilitation Center that chilly February morning, we were greeted by one of the center's directors, a tall Black woman with long braids and bright pink lips.

"I am so thrilled you all are here!" she said, clapping her hands together and ushering us to the front of the hall where we would perform. There wasn't a stage, but we were provided a microphone and a wide-open space. While we set up, the fifty residents that had joined us chatted and enjoyed sugar-free Jell-O, oatmeal cookies, and punch.

Our three Negro spirituals and our modern dance were a success. The audience members swayed, hummed, and clapped right along with us. After each applause, my body buzzed like the thrum of a church bell after it's been rung.

The monologues were the last act of our performance. As I walked up to the mic, I could feel the fake pearl necklace on my chest rising and falling with my heavy breath. I wiped my sweaty palms on the drop waist fuchsia dress Mami had let me borrow. I filled up my balloon diaphragm with as much air as I could get, closed and opened my eyes, and began.

The monologue spilled forth from my lips. Eyes moved with me left to right as I walked across the space and retold the story of how I was tired after work and didn't want to move to the back of the bus. My voice seemed to hit the back wall and bounce back into my chest. It made my whole body vibrate. I spoke clearly and with conviction, and when it was over, everyone applauded and cheered. Someone in the back even yelled: "I know that's right, girl!" My heart thumped hard, and my knees shook.

Like a little kid on her birthday, opening every gift I had wished for, I knew this was my shining moment.

At the end of our performance, an older Black woman in a wheelchair rolled up next to me. As I grabbed a couple of cookies from the snack table, she wrapped her arm around my waist. She hugged me close to her. Her paisley print dress with a lace collar brushed against my thigh. She smelled like rose soap and peppermints. Her bony fingers pressed into my hips.

"You remind me of my granddaughter," she said, nestling her head between my ribs. "You've got some real talent, young lady. And I hope you keep at it. The world needs more strong Black girls like yourself." She smiled wide. Her cherry lips trembled, and her dentures shifted in and out of place.

"Thank you, ma'am, but um, actually, I'm not Black. I'm Latina."

"Oh?" she sat back, surprised. "Well, you look Black to me!" She chuckled to herself and took a bite of her cookie.

I wasn't sure what else to say to her because all my life, I had been told I was not Black. I convinced myself she had said what she said because my performance as Rosa Parks was so convincing, she believed I was Rosa Parks that morning. I was so convincing, as Rosa Parks, she believed I was a Black woman. I took what she said as a compliment and didn't really think about it anymore after that. The adrenaline continued to pump through me as other elders from the nursing home congratulated me. It was probably one of the happiest moments of my life, and the only thing that would have made it better was if Ben had been there to see it too.

Act II

Time: Senior Year
Place: San Antonio, Texas
Character: Alice

I spent the rest of my teenage years chasing the thrill of the spotlight. Right at the end of my eighth-grade year, the Army transferred Papi to Ft. Sam Houston, San Antonio, TX. In San Antonio, like in Clarksville, there weren't any other Dominicans around me or any other Black Latinx students either. At least none that I knew of. The students at my high school, like at most any other high school, grouped themselves either by race/ethnicity or by interests, hobbies, or sports. Because my main interest was theater, that is where I found most of my friends. My theater, friends may not have shared my culture or ethnicity, but we did enjoy playing improv games and quoting lines from our favorite movies.

Drama class and the theater became my sanctuary, my safe space, the one place where I felt I really belonged. I wasn't singled out or different because I was part of an ensemble, a whole that was greater than the sum of its parts. We worked together to portray characters and build a world the audience could connect with, and the performance was the most important thing. Once those curtains opened and the lights came up, where my family was from and how or why I spoke Spanish didn't matter. No one in the audience even had to know I was Dominican. I could become anyone or anything I wanted, and the audience had to believe it. I didn't have to explain who or what I was when I was on stage. When I performed, I was not invisible, I was not different, and I could not be ignored. I took up the space I deserved and became my best self. I auditioned for every play and spent all my free time at the theater because I wanted to hold that feeling in my body and in my bones as often as I could.

Watching Ben score leading roles over and over again made me believe that with enough talent, anybody could play any role. I didn't know anything about typecasting or color-blind casting or what was or wasn't possible. I truly believed that if Ben could get roles traditionally played by white actors, then so could I. It was talent that mattered most after all, wasn't it?

But I quickly learned this was not true. My drama teachers, the Schumanns (as the drama kids called them because they functioned like one homogenous being), taught me a lot about theater and performance, but the most sobering lesson I learned from them was that it didn't matter how talented I thought I was or how talented anyone said I was, I would never "fit the part." At least, not the parts I wanted to play.

For all of high school, I chased the lead role. I memorized dozens of monologues for auditions, participated in speech competitions, and dedicated all my after-school hours to rehearsal and drama club. But it would never be enough. No matter how strong my stage presence was or how loud my voice could get, I would never be what Mr. and Mrs. Schumann wanted in a lead actress. Because what they wanted was someone who would follow orders and smile and make everyone laugh and feel good. Someone like my rival.

The quintessential "girl next door." The thin-nosed white girl with shoulder-length brown hair and perfect white teeth. You know the type: petite, smart, wears fancy clothes, and is always the first to volunteer for every improv exercise. I wanted to be white because the white girl always got the part I wanted even when I was twice as good.

For every fall play or spring one-act competition, the Schumanns always made it seem like I was the best one for the part. Before auditions, they hyped us up and boosted my confidence. They exclaimed how talented I was and that I could easily rock the lead role. But every time when I'd rush to the black box door the morning after auditions and run my fingers down the cast list, it was someone else's name at the top. Mine was always somewhere near the bottom, cast yet again as part of the ensemble. Mr. Schumann liked to say, "There are no small parts, only small actors," but the rejection always stung and swallowed me up.

When I confronted the Schumanns about their rationale behind their casting choices, they always hid their racial biases behind the tired notion that I didn't "fit the part." But "you don't fit the part" is just theater teacher code for "you are not the right skin color." For the Schumanns, the only right skin color for the lead role was white because the plays they chose to produce didn't highlight the lives and experiences of people who looked like me. I would never fit the part because I wasn't and would never be white. My hair was frizzy and struggled to fit in a wig and I was asked more than once to blow-dry and straighten it for a performance. There was also the fact that the plays they often chose were set in the forties and fifties in pre–civil rights era America and rarely starred characters whose skin was as dark as mine. I was too passionate, too opinionated, too strong, and too loud. I would never be enough because I was always "too much."

It wasn't until the spring semester of my senior year that, either out of pity for me or shame for themselves, the Schumanns decided to cast me in a lead role. Perhaps it was the complaints that I and some of my fellow theater classmates had whispered for years about the Schumanns being racist because they only ever cast white students as the lead characters. Or perhaps they really did want to give "the rest of us" a chance in the spotlight. Whatever it was, that year, the Schumanns decided to produce one more show than they usually did, and they cast all of the Black, brown, and Asian kids as the lead characters. The show they decided to produce at the end of that year was *Alice in Wonderland*.

Everyone in my varsity theater production class believed that I was the *only* person the Schumanns could cast as Alice. After almost three years of being told how "good" and "talented" I was but never being able to truly take the spotlight, everyone knew the Schumanns owed this to me before graduation.

But I had grown to be skeptical. I no longer believed I was owed or would be "given" anything. I didn't trust the Schumanns anymore, and I definitely wasn't going to feed into rumors from drama-hungry theater kids.

But they were right. The morning after auditions, when I rushed to the black box and looked up at the cast list, the first name at the top of the page was mine.

Alice—Jasminne Rosario

I squealed. I hopped up and down. Mr. Schumann came up next to me and squeezed my shoulder.

"Congrats. You earned it, kid. Now don't disappoint us." He shuffled himself to the green room to fill his coffee mug. I deflated a little. Why would he say that? Had I ever disappointed them in the past? Acting was serious business for me, and failing was not an option.

I shrugged his comment off and shimmied to class. I thought of how the theater would fill with hundreds of audience members just to see me, a Latina playing the part of one of the most famous white girls in children's literature. I felt like I had finally won. I felt like my talent had finally surpassed my looks, and now anything was possible.

As soon as I arrived at the theater that afternoon, the congratulations began. Shameka, my best friend, gave me a bear hug.

"Can you believe it! You're Alice, and I'm the Queen of Hearts! This is going to be amazing!"

"I know. I'm so excited. I can't wait." I hugged her again, then we ran down the aisle, giddy with excitement. I wanted to run home right then and there, call Ben, who was away at college, and tell him the good news. I knew he, of all people, would be happiest for me.

When Mrs. Schumann came in through the backstage door, her blonde hair swayed side to side, and her kitten heels clicked across the wooden stage. She smiled at us and said congratulations. She plopped a red crate filled with scripts on the stage and told us to grab one. I quickly pulled a script out of the crate, sat down in the first row, pulled a highlighter out of my backpack, and started highlighting my lines. The room hummed with whispers and laughter as everyone flipped through their scripts, read lines aloud, and rustled through their bags for pencils and highlighters.

I didn't talk to anyone. I focused only on the script in my hands and what it would take for me to embody the naive and lovable Alice. My highlighter lit up the pages of my script with the bright yellow glow of the summer sun.

Mrs. Schumann ran her hands through her bangs and cleared her throat. "OK, everyone, settle down. Before we get started with our read-through today, I want to talk a little bit about some of the fun and interesting design choices Mr. Schumann and I have made for this production. It's going to be super fun and really *big*!"

I thought my heart would leap out of my chest. I was desperate to know what the production ideas for this show were. Would there be a live band? Would we get elaborate costumes or wild props? How would my last and most important performance of my high school career be remembered forever? My legs bobbed up and down as I waited to hear what Mrs. Schumann had to say.

"So, what we're thinking is that this play will be performed in black light. Your costumes, props, and accessories will be white or painted with black-light paint so the audience can see your silhouette and actions. It will be fanciful and trippy like *Alice in Wonderland* is meant to be." Mrs. Schumann giggled. Clearly, she thought this was an ingenious idea.

I wasn't sure how to feel. This was not the "big" reveal I had hoped it would be. Next to me, Shameka folded her arms across her chest and spoke out without raising her hand.

"What you're saying is, no one will be able to see our faces, just our costumes and props. Right?"

"Well, you won't be completely in the dark. The audience will still see you. For example, we envision Alice wearing white gloves, and a white apron, and white shoes so her movements will really *pop* on stage."

I shifted in my seat, uncomfortable that she had chosen my character to signal out. Shameka leaned over and whispered in my ear.

"They're putting us in black light because they want to try and hide the fact that all the lead characters are Black. We can't get nothing 'round here." Shameka sucked her teeth and stuffed her script into her backpack.

A knot formed in my throat, and I bit my lip and sulked

in my seat. I had rightfully earned the lead role. No one could take away that fact. But somehow, the Schumanns had found a way to steal the joy right out of my victory. In that instant, I was sucked into a rabbit hole of self-doubt and disappointment. Would I ever be good enough? Would I ever feel seen? Suddenly, my one sacred space—the stage— was being used to render me invisible again.

Act III

Time: College
Place: Houston, Texas
Character: Ruth Younger

Despite the lack of support and encouragement from the Schumanns in high school and despite the fact that Papi didn't believe acting was a real career, I was determined to pursue my theater dreams. During my freshman year of college, I was cast in every play I auditioned for. I took as many acting and voice classes as the department would allow without majoring in theater, and I spent all my free time in the greenroom running lines, playing improv games, or preparing for the next big audition.

It didn't take long for me to realize, however, that the University of Houston's college theater department wasn't all that different from my high school. The faculty chose plays mostly written by white men that centered on white characters to appeal to a majority-white audience. All of the faculty and student directors were white, and the few Black and Latinx students that were a part of the program were usually cast as ensemble characters. Even though I had been cast in small roles that fall, by the time I went home for winter break my freshman year, I was uncertain if I would ever really have a place in my school's theater department.

"How's school and theater going?" Ben asked me at dinner one night during the Christmas holidays.

"It's alright. Lots of white kids."

"Sounds about right," Ben said with a chuckle.

"You do any shows this semester?" I asked Ben. "Mom didn't mention any to me."

"Nah. The plays they were trying to do were whack." Ben was attending a university in Dallas. It didn't have a strong theater department, and its budget was small, which led to small plays with small casts. Ben was a junior in college now, and he hadn't performed in a play in over a year. It made me sad to think he had lost his passion and his drive somehow.

"I'm doing a lot more slam poetry, though," he said, suddenly perking up. "It's a lot of fun. Going to an event tonight at Sam's Burger Joint. You wanna come?"

"Hell yeah."

I remembered Ben's speech tournaments from high school and how he won first place almost every time he performed in the poetry category. I loved reading and writing poetry almost as much as I loved theater, and a slam poetry competition sounded like exactly what I needed. That night, Ben encouraged me to sign up for the competition, too. I was hesitant at first, but Ben's "what have you got to lose" attitude convinced me to do it.

That night we each performed our own words in front

of a smoky, crowded bar filled with hoots, hollers, cheers, and jeers. Ben advanced to the final round, but I did not. Ben placed second, and I was just as in awe of him then as I was the night I saw him as Walter Younger.

After collecting his small cash prize and gift bag, a sweaty, out-of-breath Ben slumped down next to me in the booth.

"That was awesome, bro. Congrats!"

"Yeah, it was dope."

"Why haven't you been doing any shows lately, Ben?"

He shrugged and wiped his sweaty brow.

"Honestly, I really think I like slam better than theater. In slam, I get to perform the work I want to perform. Not someone else's words, ya know? It's kinda nice. I don't have to pretend to be anyone else. I don't have to work so hard to fit into who someone else wants me to be. I'm not just some minstrel show for white folks. I don't have to dance when they say dance."

Ben's words caught me by surprise. Perhaps something had happened to him in college that he was too embarrassed to talk about. Mami and Papi had been complaining about Ben's defiance and behavior lately—the mismanagement of his scholarship stipend, excessive traffic fines, and how irresponsible he was for always getting stopped by the cops. But a part of us all knew it wasn't always Ben's fault. Ben was a Black man living in Dallas, Texas, and perhaps that constant stress had finally worn him down. Or maybe it was Papi's unrealistic expectation that Ben be the perfect firstborn son. Whatever it was, it was clear that traditional theater was no longer filling Ben's spirit the way it once had. It seemed like he was finally trying to pave his own path forward.

After the holidays, feeling inspired by Ben but not ready to abandon theater myself, I joined a group of Black and Latinx students in my theater department who decided to band together to try to make a change. We wanted our voices to be heard. We wanted plays written by and for people like us to be produced on campus.

We called ourselves The Unheard Voices, and a group of us even submitted a proposal to the department to produce *A Raisin in the Sun.* It was shocking to all of us that, in the entire seventy-five-year history of the university, this canonical play had never been produced. To our surprise and delight, the panel of professors accepted our proposal.

I auditioned and was cast as Ruth Younger—Walter Lee Younger's wife. Ruth was a challenging role for me. I didn't know anything about being a married woman or getting pregnant. I was only twenty at the time and hadn't lived through any real heartache or loss. But I remembered Ben's performance of Walter when he was only fifteen, and if Ben could play Walter as a teen, then surely I could play Ruth. I learned my lines and executed my blocking and my emotional beats. I worked every day trying to find what connected me to Ruth. But everything I did felt technical and detached from Ruth's humanity.

One night, during a particularly difficult rehearsal, I had a breakdown in the greenroom. I had spent most of the rehearsal calling for lines and missing my cues. I didn't understand Ruth's character motivations or needs, and I was tired. Tired of pretending. Tired of struggling.

I was in full-on sob mode when Angela, the assistant director, sat next to me on the musty greenroom couch and gave me a tissue.

"Hey, girl. What's wrong?"

"I don't know. I'm just not feeling it tonight. I don't know if I can do this. I'm exhausted. But I know this has to be good. I know we have to show *them* that we can do this. But I'm so tired." I sniffled.

"You think we're doing this for *them*?" Angela waved wildly at the air. "Girl, we're doing this for *us*. We're not doing it for them. You are more like Ruth than you realize. Don't you think Ruth had dreams? Don't you think Ruth was tired of chasing those dreams? *You* have dreams. *You* are tired. Use your tired on stage. I know you can do it. I wouldn't have cast you in this part otherwise."

That night, during the last stretch of rehearsal, I used my tired. During the scene where Ruth has to explain to Mama that she considered getting an abortion because she's pregnant and afraid, I broke down and cried. I cried for myself. I cried for Ruth Younger. I cried for all the Black women in the world like us who have dreams that sometimes feel too far out of reach. I cried for all the things I had lost—my sense of self, my identity, my self-confidence—just to get to this moment, and I vowed to never let them go again. That night and every night on stage after that, I was able to become Ruth because I knew I already was her. Just like Ben, who, at age fifteen, had already become Walter.

I didn't know it then, but playing Ruth would, in fact, be one of the last leading roles in a traditional play I would ever have. After graduating, I would spend a couple of years attempting to make a name for myself in the local Houston theater scene, but I would quickly become disillusioned. Even in a city as diverse as Houston, the theater world failed to produce plays by people who looked like me. Even the local Black theater company would never cast me in plays because I don't think I was the kind of "Black" actress they wanted. I stopped auditioning for plays, and even though I taught middle school theater for a short two years, I would become disheartened by that as well.

I grieved this loss like heartbreak from a first love. It ached in my bones and manifested itself in nightmares of forgetting my lines onstage. Eventually, I pursued poetry and spoken word because the open mic stage was a far kinder, gentler place than the theater world would ever be. Writing my own poems and performing them in front of a crowd fueled and empowered me the way acting once had.

But it would take several years for me to get there, and on opening night of *A Raisin in the Sun*, I wasn't thinking about the future or the past or who I wasn't or wouldn't become. When the lights came up on the first scene, I was Jasminne Rosario playing Ruth Younger, and I was ready. When I looked out into the audience and saw Ben, he smiled at me like the proud big brother he was, and I knew this was my moment to shine, and that's exactly what I did. I flitted about the stage in a pink velvet robe as Ruth, as me, as every Black woman who has finally decided to take up space.

After the curtain call, I rushed out of the theater to find my family. Mami handed me a big bouquet of red and purple wildflowers, and Papi patted me on the back.

"Felicidades!" Mami said as she brushed a few curls off my forehead.

"Gracias." I smiled so hard I thought my cheeks would split open.

Ben came over to me and opened his arms wide. We had come full circle. Back to the play that started it all, except this time Ben had been watching me. I wrapped my arms around him and squeezed him tight. His voice cracked as he whispered in my ear:

"You did it, sis. You did it." We took a deep breath in together. I remembered his advice to me almost a decade before: "The core of everything is the breath." I took a deep breath as I remembered the relentless rejections, countless auditions, and grueling hours of rehearsals it took to become Rosa, and Alice, and eventually Ruth. These roles gave me the thick skin and strength I would need to pursue all my future goals and dreams both in and outside of the artistic world. I took a deep breath because I knew then that I was and had always been enough.

Invisible

Ingrid Rojas Contreras

When I married into my husband's family, I was both the enemy and enemy site. My husband and I announced our engagement and his mother cried for two days. I was brown, liberal, and immigrant, a trifecta that triggered her despair. They were white Southern Baptists living in the Middle East. Their job was to convert people. *We could be beheaded if anybody found out*, they told me, not without pride. I wasn't a Protestant and didn't keep membership in any church. My husband, Jeremiah, had left the faith, and now that he was marrying me, they had not only lost him in this life but also in the ever after.

We don't see color, Susan, my mother-in-law said, blinking away from the brown of my face.

I had just finished telling her how the color of my skin, my immigrant status, and the intersection of violence and gender were a lived politics I could not escape even if I wanted to.

Her eyes gazed at the kitchen horizon, where pots and pans were piled in the sink—presumably the apolitical whereabouts she assured existed in her mind. *We see good, we see sin. That's it.*

Susan gave me a white silk slip as a wedding gift, which she hoped I would wear to my "first night of sex" with her son. I'd already had conversations with Jeremiah and his siblings about keeping the peace. I kept a straight face and thanked her, receiving the tissue in which it was wrapped. *It's just one meal. It's just one night.* I said nothing. Once alone, I cackled at the hopeful assumption that I was a virgin. Not only was I not a virgin, but my sensuality and enjoyment of sex had also been thoroughly, spitefully, powerfully hard-won.

I am so sorry, Jeremiah said when I showed him.

It's fine. It's not like an insult. She didn't like, slap me in the face, I said, wondering if the gift had indeed been a slap in the face.

The silk ran through my hands. It was beautiful. Expensive. My thoughts short-circuited between the quality of the silk and what I saw as an implicit and disturbing demand for my purity, or worse, confirmation of the deep extent to which I went unseen. It was possible that Susan just didn't pick up on the lustiness with which I moved around in the world. It was also possible that when she said, *We don't see color,* what she meant was, *We don't see,* period.

I didn't know back then, but I know now, this is how the worst of whiteness works. Insults are tied up in acts of kindness. Judgments are laced under cover of benevolence. No harm done is ever done on purpose. There is an excuse for everything.

You can grow fond of people, even of people for whom you are invisible.

I liked the way his father, Jim, spoke of his youth. In a

bemused whisper, he told me that he drank and smoked
weed and listened to the Beatles—the devil's music—when
he was young and that he "said anything to get a girl in
bed." He confessed these things as if they were the worst
things a human being was capable of. I respected that the
harm of using a woman's romantic notions to mislead her
into sex was something to consider with gravity. It was an
insight that eluded many "feminist" men.

I was moved when his mother asked ahead of my visits
what food I liked, then spent hours in the kitchen trying to
create a meal I would enjoy. The bed where I was to sleep
was always dressed in fresh linen, and there were thoughtful
touches. Susan knew I got cold, so there were extra blankets
set out. She knew I was a writer and always received me
with a new notebook and a pen.

Yet I can't say they liked anything about me, though I
am sure they tried. I don't want children, I am pro-choice
and career-oriented, and at the time, I worked through a
city program to run and teach writing classes to undocumented immigrant youth, who they thought of as criminals.

I feel like we don't really know you, they said, after
years of knowing me. For once, I agreed with them. We
had spent countless nights together, solved jigsaw puzzles,
watched movies, delighted at delicious meals, and though
I wasn't hiding who I was, somehow they came away feeling I was a stranger.

I used to think that neglecting to remember details about
a person belonged to a minor class of offenses, like mixing
up a name or forgetting someone's trade. It belied a lack of
attention. What is the harm, after all, of someone mistaking

you for a virgin? But unawareness is not the same as refusing to see. There is plenty of harm in looking in a person's direction and blurring your eyes until you see what you want to see, or until you see nothing at all.

The cost of being loved so poorly was the constant aftermath of rage.

Over the ten years we had known each other, Susan had asked about babies. I consistently answered in the negative, as in I never wanted any; nonetheless, one day in 2016, as she and Jim arrived at our apartment to spend some summer days together, she had brought me a gift. She had sewn me a baby quilt. She stitched it, she gushed, while vividly imagining the baby it would one day enshroud.

I stared at her, considering what to do. In my childhood house in Bogotá, my mother had worked, like her father before her, as a curandera. Her consulting office was in the attic, and all kinds of people frequented our house, seeking her healing and divination. What Susan described was what we would call witchcraft without hesitation. The creation of an object with the impassioned intention of superimposing your will over another's was a dangerous and violent thing to do.

Over the years of answering Susan's question about babies, I had allowed my replies to become increasingly graphic and imagistic, hoping to finally lay the subject to rest. *Every time I see a baby,* I had told her last, *I feel my ovaries shrink and retract.* I had made a limp clawing gesture with my hands and drew them slowly to my chest to convey how little I wanted to be a mother. It wasn't a failure of language, nor was it an innocence about the violence of her gift. Susan simply did not want to hear or acknowledge what I wanted for myself.

I can't accept it, I told Susan and reiterated my desire to be childfree. She wanted me to keep the baby blanket nonetheless. In case I changed my mind.

I won't.

You might.

I still refused, and she was visibly hurt. A few hours later, I overheard her crying to my husband in an adjacent room. *Why is Ingrid so difficult? I was just trying to do a nice thing.*

Why couldn't I receive a gift that had obviously been so time-consuming even if I disagreed with it and didn't want it and it functioned as a means for manipulation?

What she really was asking was: Why wasn't I white?

Politeness and sparing someone's feelings are not a priority for me—I was raised to care about having my own ambitions for my life and body respected, and I was encouraged to have my own back.

Anger is a powerful language in my family, one through which we make one another understand how we want to be treated, what roads we won't follow, what things we won't tolerate. Our anger teaches us and our beloveds how we want to be loved.

We are funny about it too. *Su madre!* my mother would say to me at random when I passed her in the halls of our house in Bogotá. *What?* I protested. *I didn't do anything!*

Mami narrowed her eyes. *That was for in the event you were* thinking *about disrespecting me.*

I waited many years to tell her that in these aggrieved escapades, she was only insulting herself.

I grew up watching Mami and the tías ignite with anger the second they were disrespected. We spent our vacations with Mami's extended family in the northeastern part of the country, in Cúcuta. It was hot year-round, and I subsisted on the avocadoes and pomegranates that grew in my grandmother's backyard.

One night, I remember, one of Mami's brothers held up an empty glass to her and barked an order: *Go in the kitchen and fill this with ice.* Mami could have scrunched up her face, showed distaste, said hotly, *I don't appreciate your tone,* as I imagine a person from the United States might have, but we're Colombian, and anger is a language we are fluent in. We know exactly what is beneath the tumult of emotion, and we use the heat of our words to signal there is a line we don't want crossed. So Mami advanced on her brother with fury, snatched the glass, threw it to the dark of the jungle, and said *there* was his ice. It was a lesson he took, I observed at the time because he didn't talk to her like that again, though that night, he laughed and called her a snake, he couldn't believe he had forgotten, and he warned others to be careful of her bite. And that was the point. To treat her nicely, or not at all.

Jeremiah's family, by contrast, is deeply conflict-averse. A newcomer to their dynamic, I knew there were things that went unaddressed, and I doubted they would ever be dealt with at all. It is a quality also endemic to this country.

Susan and Jim were people who, in their own children's recollections, never raised their voices, left rooms before saying anything hurtful, would a million times rather deal with conflict by addressing a Higher Spirit than having a face-to-face conversation.

I tried to explain these cultural differences to Susan and Jim, but they didn't understand, and things only got worse.

Soon, our conversations devolved into echolocations of each other's intent.

Susan hadn't meant anything as we were walking around in the Mission District in San Francisco, and she furrowed her brow and exclaimed, *There's so many Asians!*

I tried pointing out how strange it would be for me to say, *There's so many whites!* It implied that I wasn't expecting to share space with them, or that I was inferring they didn't belong in the United States, or that I was ignorant of their belonging.

Maybe you're just looking to be offended, Susan said.

Jim and Susan were staying with us for a week, and micro-aggressions were the water in which we lived. A conversation with them was a journey through a hall of smoke and mirrors. Susan had just been making an innocent observation. I was reading into things. I was unfair. I needed to lighten up. There was nothing that serious about making a descriptive remark. I bent over backward trying to rationalize their offenses. Maybe I was too sensitive.

As I went to my work with immigrant youth and returned, with the passing of days, Susan and Jim's interest in what happened in my classroom, what my kids were learning, what kind of poetry they wrote, morphed into their demanding to know how these children had entered the country. I declined to disclose that information but told them they were asylum seekers. Susan talked about the dangers of the MS-13. I asked her to clarify why she was bringing up a Los Angeles gang and tilted my head and felt my own cheeks grow hot with outrage. This seemed to hurt her, that I could stew with so much anger, you could read every inch of it on my face, and then Jim began to tell me that a woman owed obedience to all the fathers in her life—God, the husband, the church—and then, like both Jim and Susan were having a conversation in another dimension, Susan told me that they didn't care I was brown, or an immigrant, or obsessed with work, but she wanted me to know that estrangement from someone was a series of choices, they were small, and one day you woke up divorced.

I looked to Jeremiah, who seemed not only as shocked as I was by their words and their irrational sequence; he also looked scared and helpless. He was as conflict-averse as his parents. My anger grew.

When you walk into a fragile house, as a daughter-in-law, you're not supposed to blow the structure. You're not supposed to bring more harm than what already lives there.

I had met Jeremiah when Susan and Jim had cut him off for moving to Chicago to go to art school, which they viewed as a hotbed of devilry. Exiling him hurt them more than it did him, they said, as, in the eyes of God, it ensured his damnation. Jeremiah and I spent that holiday season together—he had no home to go to, and I couldn't travel back to Colombia because I had no money for the ticket.

I saw firsthand the pain that their exclusion caused and I imagined, at this moment, he was there again. A disconsolate pain lived in the space where he feared his parents might exile him once more. These were people who had no way of communicating their anger, and I couldn't use my language of anger since it would surely be misinterpreted as actual violence. This is what I told myself as I left the table without saying anything more. I left early every day to go write somewhere else, and I didn't return home until very late at night, or I spent the night elsewhere.

Your parents are racist, I told Jeremiah and his siblings later that winter when we all got together in Michigan, where Jeremiah's sister lived.

No, they all said, laughing it off. *They're just . . . ignorant.*

They are very racist, I said, citing my arsenal of examples from when Susan and Jim had visited us in California that summer, as well as from years prior. And while I was heard, my observations were cast into doubt. Susan and Jim were well-meaning, naive, and unenlightened when it came to race. If they were educated in the right way, I was told, they would steer away from racist language and actions. This was exhausting, too. It wasn't just Susan and Jim. Whiteness itself doesn't like to look at or recognize whiteness. The inability to bear witness, to dwell in what feels uncomfortable, travels down the line. It carries over, like a fucked-up arithmetic. And for this family of five, being conflict-averse meant that they all chose to avert their eyes away from the things that might invite discord. They could not see, and I could not get any of them to understand, however hard I tried, that discord can, in turn, invite justice.

By 2015, Susan and Jim had completed their missionary assignment in the Middle East and moved back to Arizona, where Susan's parents lived. They voted for Trump. It was only then that Jeremiah and his siblings were forced to confront who their parents are and what views they might espouse. *I think our parents are racist!* they said to each other in shock.

I can still remember the sick-to-my-stomach feeling of election night. I had plans to go to a DADA party, which promised me robotic antics and political parody. My friend Ken and I had wandered into a bar where a dim room was filled with balloons. The incoming results were projected onto a wall. I was feeling festive and in the mood for an intellectual conversation about the effects of reality television on politics. It's hard to pinpoint the exact moment grief began to sink in—slow, then quick. I rode a downward spiral of despair, knowing there would be even more deportations now, that if racism and sexism were legitimized by the office of the presidency, the atrocious and violent things that had been brewing were now definitely coming our way. I felt sick and wiped tears from my cheeks at a table where two artists from France were listening to my fears, telling me in French, *Courage, courage.*

The next day my in-laws sent an email. The subject line was all lowercase: *thoughts.* They guessed we were disappointed by the election results. The KKK had just gone on a victory parade, and on their website, a photo of Trump was accompanied by the message: "Racial greetings from the Loyal White Knights of the Ku Klux Klan." What I was feeling was closer to mortal fear. Susan and Jim did not apologize for their vote, but they expressed sorrow at being the older generation that gave the younger generation its presidential choices. They declared that the election results had inspired them to jump into action—but what they meant was that they were going to start praying for Trump. They had prayed for Obama too, *but not daily.* They suggested we respect the election results and then quoted a Bible verse: "Romans 13:1. There is no authority except that which God has established."

I composed the angriest email of my life. They had a double morality, I told them. They glossed over malevolence. They were implicated in whatever horrors came next. *You've elected a man on the razor-thin hope that he is not who he seems to be over the bodies of gay people, people of color, women, immigrants, and Muslims. And this I cannot, do not, and will never respect.*

Jeremiah and his siblings wrote livid emails of their own, and for once, I didn't feel alone in my reading of their parents. It was a relief. It hadn't all been in my head.

After the election, there was not a lot of generosity I could muster for those who had put us in a dangerous predicament. The only kindness I could offer to my partner was to show up as a sign of respect for the people who raised him. We arrived for the holidays at their home in Arizona. Nobody had talked outside of the exchange of aggrieved emails that had been lobbed back and forth for weeks. Showing up was a token of my theoretical belief in people and not in their mistakes. But I refused to stay in Susan and Jim's house. I refused to go to their church. I was angry, and I would not pretend otherwise.

I realized that my believing in people and *not* their mistakes, too, had been a mistake. Jeremiah's family did what they always did: they ignored conflict and did not acknowledge any harm done. I observed them hug and talk about the plane ride as if we had not spent the last forty-eight hours airing our grievances. They smiled, I could see, through their anger and disappointment, passing plates, asking for the salt.

I interrupted a conversation between my husband and his brother: "Hey, remember when your parents voted for Trump?"

They snorted, then grimaced, remembering their own pain. The anger settled on their faces, then passed, like swift bad weather. The nightmare of their parents' votes safely stowed far away in the reaches of their minds, they picked up where they left off: the dark existential spirituality of David Lynch films. This was whiteness too—the untouchable quality of their privilege that allowed them to sweep everything, in one second, under the rug.

I inhaled and held my breath in frustration and felt profoundly unsafe, scared, and alone. I didn't understand why Jeremiah and his siblings all thought that if they pushed against their parents' views, Susan and Jim would end up exiling them all. They didn't perceive this as emotional manipulation. They had decided as a group that what they needed was to try to heal by being together as a family, as they had been before, no matter the cost.

I was the cost. Angry and isolated, at their dining table. I was understanding but not forgiving. Jeremiah and his siblings assured me they were on my side. How they could see what was happening. They had my back. I went back and forth, convinced they did, and they knew they did not. While I was horrified that my community and the communities I cared about were in danger, and my in-laws had been instrumental in that result, Jeremiah's siblings did not see this pain as their own. They talked about their parents abstractly, telling one another, *One day they'll realize they were on the wrong side of history.*

After dinner, the family played a card game, which I declined to join. I watched the violence of their silence unfold.

I took out my phone and sent a forlorn text in Spanish to my mother: "They're pretending nothing happened. I am so angry. And nobody here knows how to make a scene or would support a scene if I created one."

In seconds, my mother commiserated: "I would have made a scene *so* long ago."

"What would you have done?"

She described wine thrown into people's faces, plates shattered, maybe a few things set on fire. Ah, anger. I smiled. I nestled with my phone and read and reread Audre Lorde's essay on anger, and that was the company I kept. "Every woman has a well-stocked arsenal of anger potentially useful against the oppressions which brought that anger into being," Audre Lorde wrote. "Focused with precision, anger can become a powerful source of energy serving progress and change. And when I speak of change, I do not mean a simple switch of positions or a temporary lessening of tensions, nor the ability to smile or feel good. I am speaking of a basic and radical alteration in those assumptions underlining our lives."

I wanted nothing more than to alter the harmful assumptions ruling my life.

I told Jeremiah that I had only shown up to this holiday get-together because I was giving his parents a chance to make things right. And so far, they hadn't.

You're fucking scary when you're angry, Jeremiah told me. *Do you think my parents are going to want to talk to you? They were afraid of you before. Let me try to bring it up my way.*

At the end of our stay, I received a lukewarm apology, and it felt good. I took what little his parents were able to give. But everything was a reminder of how inaccessible true closure was still. After apologizing, Susan said, *I know how you feel, I just want you to know.* She swooped in for a hug. She spoke into my hair: *I myself have been at the end of reverse racism.*

I know Jeremiah's parents and I lived in different realities. We said the word *law* and meant different things. I said cages, and they said the rumors were false. I said racism, and they brought up identity politics and ethnic activists. I said refugees, and they used the word "illegals." And they saw ANTIFA as masked delinquents sowing chaos and violence everywhere.

The United States of America was then and is now living through a time that makes whiteness visible, even to those who lived their whole lives willingly ignoring what it entails. As the months passed, I pondered the question: What is there to forgive? When you join a family peripherally, by marriage—what, if anything, is owed to you? What do you owe back? When the Charlottesville white nationalist march occurred in the summer of 2017, and a white supremacist terrorist drove into a crowd of counter-protesters, killing one person and injuring eighteen others, Jim said: *But there was violence on both sides.*

I was owed, in the least, never hearing a comment like that.

I had the realization, at long last, that I was in a toxic relationship.

We were in a cycle together. I felt Jim and Susan had betrayed their own beliefs, and I was angry at being misled into believing they had morals. I wanted to prove them wrong. They wanted to prove me wrong. What I wanted most of all was to get to the bottom of the mystery: Was I crazy, or were they?

I didn't see Susan and Jim in person again until the winter of 2018 when Jeremiah and I traveled to see them.

Our time apart had made the tensions come closer to the surface. Jim was terrified about what the media termed "the migrant caravan," which was a group of Central Americans fleeing climate change, violence, and war, but who he saw as gang-affiliated criminals. I tried to tell Susan and Jim that seeking asylum was not a crime, that that's what the process was at any border of any country in the world.

Jim told me that he believed in borders, then asked if I was "illegal."

You think I'm undocumented? My first reaction was confusion. I had acquired my green card through marriage to their son, and it wasn't a small thing, either. I was close to having to leave the country before we decided to get married. It had been a relief to find a way to stay in a place where I was starting to remake my life.

I had traveled internationally before with Jim and Susan; they had witnessed an immigration officer stamp my passport. Even if they had been inattentive then, a favorite story of theirs was how I had been pulled aside while going through customs in England, and an older white woman had spoken to me loudly and slowly, and when I responded in perfect English, she still addressed Jeremiah instead of me, *Your little friend here needs a visa to enter.* Jim and Susan had repeated the phrase to me, laughing, *"Your little friend!" I just think that's so funny, "your little friend here"! Isn't that funny?*

My second reaction was alarm. The implication of Jim's question was that I could not be invested in other people's well-being unless I held a personal stake in the threat.

My memory was long. I remembered all the barbs hiding beneath the slick veneer of good intentions, the stubbornness of their own ignorance, the aggressive insistence on being perfectly informed and in the right. I remember vividly as Jim very seriously sliced his arm through the air and said, "Climate change is not real," and how a few years later, once the religious publications he subscribed to started to report on it, sat me down to explain what climate change was.

That night, I let it go. I had just arrived, and I wanted to try to extend kindness to my in-laws. I explained the laws of immigration and the different types of immigrants. Then I went to bed. I was trying very hard to make a relationship with Jeremiah's parents work because I wanted

Jeremiah to not have to be afraid of his parents abandoning him. I felt debilitated and fatigued, and still, I doled out explanations and tried to share what I knew.

The next day, I was considering that just because I could put up with a lot didn't mean I should when Jim inclined over the dining table to hand me a book—*Full of facts*, said he, *which lay clear, sound, scientific arguments about why immigration is bad for the economy, scientific progress, and Christian values.*

A whole set of dishes prepared by Susan sat waiting in the kitchen, with some still in the oven, and I inhaled and took the book. I didn't point out the irony of him thinking that I had something to learn about immigration when they had so obviously not understood at all what it meant to be an asylum seeker just a day before. I turned the book over to read who had written it, and then, painfully, I had to ask, "Do you know what eugenics is?"

"Of course," Jim said, his mouth firm in a line, into which I read resentment over the insinuation that he did not.

"It says here the author is pro-eugenics and started a Eugenics Institute?"

"It's a *factual* book. It's scientific."

I stared at him now with attention. "Explain eugenics to me."

He spoke of things that had happened long ago, things the Nazis had done in Germany, and sterilizations which had happened in the United States but which had nothing to do with now, and definitely not with him, who I kept meanly accusing of racism and who, as it happened, had no racist bone in his body. Susan nodded along to her husband's words and stared at me in silence. She seemed both perplexed by my reaction and like she was waiting for my misreading of her husband's intentions to sink in.

"You think this is okay to give this book to me?"

"I don't see why I can't give you a *book.*"

I gathered my things, my phone, and my sweater and went into the room where I was staying. Beyond the hurt that ran through my body like poison, I felt an acute relief. After eleven years of not knowing whether I had been too judgmental or sensitive, now I knew I had not been paranoid. Here, finally, was real proof that I was not inventing things. Susan and Jim held racist beliefs. These beliefs were stowed in parts of themselves they deemed nonexistent, and from that nonexistent place came the very real vitriol that hurt me in every interaction we had.

What it comes down to is this:

You come to know what eugenics means, and you either recoil at the mention of it, or you do not. You either see the problem with buying a book on immigration written by a man who is pro-eugenics or you do not. You either see the cruelty of giving that book to your immigrant daughter-in-law or you do not. Jim and Susan's lack of disgust at eugenics told me all I need to know. Here was something undeniably immoral. Here was undeniable evidence of how much I, and people like me, were discardable to them. There was no other layer beneath this. This is who they were.

I did not need something worse to happen. I blinked once, and just like that, I knew I didn't want them in my life anymore, not across the table, not at the other end of a phone, not in the same house, ever. I didn't have to stay, and I could not, in fact, stay for one second longer. I began to pack.

On the other side of the door, I heard Jeremiah argue with his parents. After a few minutes, when he came in to see if I was okay and what we should do, I told him, *I am a danger to myself and others, if I don't leave now I'm going to burn down your parents' house.* Jeremiah called me a cab. I saw that he was terrified of leaving his parents at that moment, and I told him he should stay. I had never broken up with in-laws before. How was it done? It turned out to be simple. Once my car was outside waiting to take me to the airport, I came out dragging my suitcase and informed them I was leaving. I thanked them for raising their son. Jim was drying dishes with a rag. He was actually whistling, refusing to face me, while Susan stared at me with tears running down her face. I said, *I cannot and do not want to have a relationship with you any longer, anymore, at all,* and then I walked out.

The decision seems easy now, like everything else that I examine in hindsight. I can't believe I didn't leave sooner. Which is what everyone who has left a toxic relationship says.

In the cab, I felt a lightness and freedom I had not felt in years, and I realized that all this time, what I yearned for was someone to give me permission to leave. For eleven years, I had awaited confirmation that I was living in a perpetually abusive dynamic, but since no one had confirmed my perception of reality, I had overstayed. I told myself, *Never again.* I did not need permission to leave a dynamic I felt was abusive. All that leaving required was myself validating my own reality. I called my sister, crying at the airport. She was elated that I had finally ended my relationship with Jeremiah's parents. I didn't know why I hadn't heard her voice of support sooner. I sat in the airport bar in Mesa, Arizona, where the bartender heard me cry and laugh and served me free drink after free drink. I had not known how unhappy I was, I told him, how weighed down under the boulder of filial obligation until I said goodbye forever. I told him everything, and even this bartender who I had known for one second was proud of me. By the end, I had made him cry with my crying.

To this day, Susan and Jim say that my walking out that day was the worst thing anyone has ever done to them. I was rude beyond reason—I, a wrecking ball to their well-being and unity.

I wish they could understand what I know—willful ignorance is violent.

During the four years that Trump was in power, many people died and were irreparably, profoundly harmed. Immigrant women suffered hysterectomies that were done without their consent in ICE facilities. Families continued to be separated. Children were forcibly injected with psychoactive drugs to quiet their despair. A deadly virus spread across prisons and ICE concentration camps.

Violence begins with language or lack of it. If you insist that something doesn't exist, it is in that darkness that calamity slips in.

If children kept in cages at the border is a lie, how can

the news that COVID-19 is spreading like wildfire in those concentration camps be seen and understood?

Silence and inattention allow for other crimes, and these crimes—intrinsically entwined with willful ignorance—cannot exist without either, which makes the way white people avert their eyes criminal. White people live with dangerous pockets that remain unseen, uncharted, ignored. Nobody has ever demanded that they learn to identify their fear, comb through it, see it for what it is, face the reality of where emotion fails to match the truth, and come to terms with what that means.

I know that both Susan and Jim voted for Trump in 2020. After not being in touch for a whole year, they sent me a gift in the mail—as if time was all I needed to see that they had not meant what they had said or done.

What do we owe each other?

I know that I do not owe them my inner peace. I do not owe them purity, vulnerability, heat, or the sum of my life that I build up around me in a frenzy so it can spill over in abundance to all my beloveds. I get to choose who I love and who I extend my vulnerability toward.

I think that I owed Susan and Jim my attention and understanding, which I gave and which they have. I am not even angry anymore. But this does not mean they belong in my life. I wish them well. I hope that someday they are able to confront the harm they've done and keep from doing more. I hope they become better people.

I don't need to be part of their path to redemption.

Now, what I want is to be what I had always been to them: invisible.

Tell them to never send me a gift again, I said to Jeremiah. *I don't want them to ask after me, wonder how I am, anything at all. When I say I don't want a relationship, that's exactly what I mean. Tell them I want them to think I'm invisible. Tell them I want them to think I don't exist.*

Abuela's Greatest Gift

Janel Martinez

I had to mentally prepare myself for my 2009 trip to Honduras.

While I enjoyed catching up with family over hudutu, endless glasses of freshly squeezed guanábana juice, slipping into an afternoon nap in a hammock, or daily walks on the beach, this particular visit home would be different. My abuela Gregoria wouldn't physically be there to greet us when the truck pulled up in front of my family's Ciriboya home.

A year after her passing, my family traveled from the Bronx, as well as different parts of Honduras, to my father's hometown for her beluria. It is customary for Garinagu to honor the life of a deceased loved one a year after transition. Arriving a couple of days before the big celebration of her spirit, I watched my father, aunts, uncles, and cousins map out logistics surrounding food, lodging, and music. The day- and nightlong celebration was breathtaking. Tears came to my eyes as I watched a procession of women, a mix of aunts, cousins, and community members, dressed in beautiful traditional garb, singing and swaying as they honored her legacy. The procession moved from the main road, turning into our yard and settling into the house. No one stood still as the chanting, drums, and conch shell horn melded into a harmonious, rhythmic beat.

Then, punta began.

The movement of hips and feet in unison with the drum and horn—you couldn't tell me I wasn't witnessing divinity in its truest form. I watched as my cousins took turns in entering the circle that formed, moving in honor of our latest ancestor. Though I felt a pull to join them, I remained on the outskirts of the circle, admiring their ability to surrender to that spiritual call. Self-doubt tugged at me. Of course, I've danced punta, but my thoughts double Dutch between entering the circle and staying in my physical and cultural place. The complexities of my identity—US-born, "native tongue" English (not Spanish nor Garifuna), with a handful of visits to Honduras stamped into my navy blue passport—were affirmed at that moment. Abuela's ancestral welcome was an invitation for me, too, to step further into my full self: A Black woman. An Afro-Indigenous woman. A woman with roots in Honduras by way of forcible exile from St. Vincent and the Grenadines. A descendant of West and Central African maroons who fought tirelessly for their freedom, no matter the land they called home.

Many people are unfamiliar with Garinagu, but we have a unique and complex history that involves attempts to enslave, imprison, exile, and displace our Afro-Indigenous community. The exact year is subject to debate, but my ancestors escaped and survived slave ships wrecked off the coast of St. Vincent and the Grenadines in the 1600s.

While residing in St. Vincent, or Yurumein, West and Central African descendants mixed with the Caribbean island's Arawak and Carib populations, forming the community known as Black Carib, or Garifuna. After the British were given St. Vincent in a treaty with the French in 1763, Black Carib resistance intensified. Chief Joseph Chatoyer, or Satuye, led an ongoing battle (the First Carib War) with the British, which resulted in the signing of a peace treaty in 1773. Though Britain signed, they retracted and the Second Carib War, led by Satuye, began in 1795. Sadly, the freedom fighter was reportedly killed on the first day of the war. Garinagu were enraged (and rightfully so), fighting more fiercely and gaining ground until they were defeated in 1797. Five thousand Garinagu were exiled, and the survivors arrived in Roatán, the largest of Honduras's Bay Islands, on April 12, 1797. The 2,000 that survived migrated to mainland Honduras, Belize, Guatemala, and Nicaragua.

Garinagu remain along Central America's Caribbean coast. However, migration has resulted in Garifuna communities in several US cities like Houston, Los Angeles, Chicago, New Orleans, and New York City—home to the largest Garifuna population outside of Central America. I'm proud to call my hometown a vital center for us. Estimates place the number of Garinagu in NYC at more than 200,000, with the majority residing in the South Bronx. Whether gathered at Crotona Park, where you can find kékè, pan de coco, durudia, or a number of baked Garifuna treats for sale or large family gatherings in somebody's apartment, I witnessed the many ways we've created a home away from home.

My most vivid memories involve food and dishes that connect Honduras to the place I grew up calling home in the Bronx. Saturday mornings were a favorite of mine, not because I was off from school (though that was nice) or I'd have extra time to play, but because of the hudutu my parents religiously made on this day. I'd watch, beaming with excitement, as my parents worked in tandem to create this traditional Garifuna dish. The hiss of the kingfish as it first hit the oil hinted at what was to come, followed by the distinctive fragrance. My mother would stand over the pan frying or tending to the coconut stew, or falmo, on the stove, and my father would boil the plátanos—green and one ripe plantain—then set them aside to cool in our kitchen before he pounded them in the hana.

Thump. Thump. Thump.

A signature sound of the hudutu-making process as the mortar hits the plátanos in the wooden pestle. While this was happening, bowls were filled with stew, then set on the table, and the final touch was the ball of mashed plátanos placed at the center of the table. There was little conversation as my father, mom, brother, and I enjoyed the smooth, mashed plantain in our flavorful stew, a side plate accruing a collection of fish bones.

We wouldn't always have falmo. Other times it would be fish or even chicken stew. If my maternal abuelita prepared it, she'd make it with crabs. The marriage between the crab and coconut stew, with the aroma of onions, garlic, and black pepper, was as alluring as the scent of freshly made tortillas. As a child, seeing my father take out the oil, flour, and salt from the cabinet signaled another favorite dish would be on the menu. There's an art to setting the dough in balls and later patting them into a circle before they hit the heat. Seeing the fresh stack of tortillas on the counter was a source of joy. My abuelita Dominga's durudia, tortillas with coconut milk, were always a treat; to this day, she'll save me at least one if I'm coming over. Biting into a warm tortilla provides flashbacks to Honduras, eating the freshest tortillas at breakfast with mantequilla — crema, not to be confused with butter — or actual butter.

During one of my visits to Honduras, I watched how the ereba, or casabe — that I saw so often appear from a plastic-wrapped suitcase — was made. Though I missed the gathering, washing, grounding, and straining of the yuca, I caught what I thought was the most exciting part: the baking. Witnessing my aunt spread the yuca flour into a circle on a large, black, hot stove, smoothing and flattening it with el aduguley, a wooden slab; brushing the excess flour away with a baisawa, a small, hand-held broom. While it didn't fully crystalize then, important moments like that would be crucial in my overall understanding of our oral traditions, history, and connection to our ancestral lands.

Language was also a big part of my understanding of Garifunaidad. Many expect, given my last name and Honduran roots, that I speak fluent Spanish. However, I was raised hearing Garifuna salutations like "buiti binafi" (hello/good morning), "buiti guñoun" (good night), and "ida biña?" (how are you?) at every turn. My parents spoke Garifuna to each other, to a majority of my family in the

States and back home. Abuelita spoke it with my mother, aunts, and at home in the Bronx to my grandfather. I don't speak Garifuna fluently, but I can often pick up the general gist of conversations. My brother and I always laugh when we remember our mother's favorite phrase, "Maganba di tu" (you don't listen (f)). When we heard it, we knew we were in trouble. But, she'd also affectionately say, "dai haruga, numada" (tomorrow, my friend), before closing my bedroom door each night.

That's the beauty of a home. It's not perfect, but the safety and love that exist there are innately understood. No excessive explanations are needed. I often felt that, and still do, in my parents' Bronx home, my abuelitos' crib, or amid family in our ancestral home of Honduras. It's when I left home that the questions, expectations, and preconceived notions emerged.

Now, I have the vocabulary to unapologetically articulate who I am. However, it's taken me decades to get to this particular place. Of course, I've always known I was a Black girl. Beyond my very textured 'fro, which my mother somehow masterfully slicked into braids fastened by bo bos on wash day, and medium-brown complexion, there were experiences that only Black girls could relate to. At an early age, I learned that my girlhood had limits outside of the safety of my own home. Women in my life providing instructions on how to conceal my budding curves; howtos on dodging inappropriate gestures from boys and men; notes on the importance of taking up space, but not too much; and periodic check-ins to ensure physical boundaries were not crossed. While most girls can relate, this is heightened for Black girls who are seen as much older and hypersexual from a young age. The policing of our agency is a constant reminder of how we're viewed within society. It doesn't stop us, but the attempts to quiet us or minimize our existence are harmful.

One of my earliest memories of having my identity policed happened when I was in grade school. It was the first day, and the teacher asked the class to go around the room to introduce ourselves. When it was time for me to stand up and introduce myself, I did. Shortly after I sat down, my classmate, whose parents were from Spain, turned and asked me, "What are you?"

I replied, "Spanish." (For the record, today, I would never identify as a language or a descendant of Spain, but it was a go-to response for those of us with roots in a Spanish-speaking country.)

"No, you're not," my classmate responded. I was both shocked and confused that this kid, who was neither a friend nor a family member, felt he could tell me who I am. We went back and forth, yet he refused to accept me as "Spanish."

That was when it hit me. If my last name and explanation weren't enough, it could only be one thing: my skin tone. I'm Black, and there's no room for Blackness within Hispanidad or Latinidad. While my understanding of Latinidad was both Black and/or Indigenous, as a white Spaniard, he—and society—didn't have to acknowledge that.

That incident left me feeling upset and flustered. My mother had known this day, and so many others like it, would come; so, she always said, "If anyone asks you what you are, you tell them you're a Black Hispanic." While I don't use the term Hispanic to describe myself today, her words affirmed my existence and were my reminder to educate others that there are Black folks in Latin America. In fact, when you look at recipes rich in root vegetables or musical genres like rumba or reggaetón, Black and Indigenous Latin Americans have contributed significantly to Latinx culture, yet Black Latinxs are frequently erased from Latinidad.

Existing at the intersection of Latin American, Caribbean, Black, and Indigenous identity, I've always been hyper-aware of how I view myself and how other people view me, including the areas where the two didn't align. I found the language to support my experience as an undergrad at Syracuse University, but learning about Black identity in Paris, France, during my African American Studies summer seminar abroad connected me to the term Afro-Latina. Hundreds of Google searches later, I found an identifier that centered my Blackness and acknowledged my Latin American descendancy. My study abroad experience also empowered me to center my Garifunaidad. While it's always been a prominent part of my existence, it's taken me decades to really unearth Garifuna history, and I take the utmost pride in sharing it whenever I can. Whether proudly identifying as Garifuna or reporting on our ethnicity and culture, and, more specifically, members of our community, I do so because I want the next generation of Garinagu to be proud of our existence, resilience, and power. Even if we're not shown prominently in the media, we matter.

Like many Black girls of Latin American descent in the US, growing up, I didn't see my entire self in the pages of magazines, as the main character in sitcoms and movies, or news anchors in either Spanish-language or English programming. I found myself feverishly researching artists, actors, and public figures—and when I finally put two and two together, identifying Zaria of *The Parent 'Hood,* played by Reagan Gomez-Preston; *The Fresh Prince of Bel-Air*'s Tatyana Ali; and singer-songwriter Kelis (her '06 *Vibe Vixen* cover story where she revealed her Puerto Rican roots is a personal favorite) as Afro-Latinas, I knew there were more public figures who identified similarly. Panama-born, Brooklyn-raised author and journalist Veronica Chambers was my first example of a Black Central American in the media. Her 2000 *Essence* article, "The Secret Latina," struck a chord with me, serving as a much-needed reminder that our stories are relevant and worth telling.

"You could meet me and not know I was of Latin heritage," she wrote. ". . . Latinos were not quick to claim me. Latinos can be as racist as anybody else, favoring blue-eyed *rubias* over *negritas* like me." I felt every word as the younger me knew that feeling all too well. I saw myself in Veronica's narrative, but as a Garifuna woman, I still yearned to see my Afro-Indigenous identity in print, online, or on-screen. My family reflected the full range of Blackness, so why wasn't that shown?

After majoring in magazine journalism and working in the industry right out of school, the gaps consumed me. As an intern at a well-known, now defunct publication, I was eager to learn the ins and outs of the magazine industry. My first-day nerves subsided as I got to know the editors better and began working on assignments for both print and digital. I even dabbled in the fashion and beauty department, which was a dream of mine. Though I gained an incredible amount of experience, one conversation solidified the notion that Afro-Latinxs are an afterthought in Latinx-centered editorial content and advertising. In my editor's office, I sat across from her and asked, "Is there an opportunity to have more Afro-Latinas featured?" The response I received alluded to the magazine and online editorial content, which barely scratched the surface in terms of inclusion. Though I felt dismissed, I naively expected the day would come where there would be greater representation in traditional Latinx media. The idea of starting something to fill the void crossed my mind, but I was optimistic that this publication, or another one, would beat me to it given their resources. However, I was reminded that in order to see the Black Latinx experience in a way that authentically resonates with our diverse community, we'd have to create it. I'd witnessed the women in my family—my 'lita, mother, and aunts—create opportunities for themselves and our family, so I knew that spirit has always been in me.

Once my internship ended, I took a position at an African American legacy outlet that focused on entrepreneurship and business. I interviewed hundreds of entrepreneurs, innovators, and creatives who had an idea and decided to execute it. That was my sign of moving forward with my idea to launch *Ain't I Latina?* I didn't have a name but felt drawn to marry my love of storytelling with a passion for highlighting Black Latinx women. It was clear how other women of the diaspora were drawn to organic conversations that centered us, which was evident via social media, particularly Tumblr, Twitter, and Facebook, and very specific websites like BoriquaChicks.com that were emerging. The digital space cut out the middleman—media executives, producers, and editors—providing an opportunity for content creators like myself to share our unfiltered perspectives. Settling my fear and uncertainty, I pushed the *Ain't I Latina?* Twitter and Facebook pages live. After going live on social media, AintILatina.com launched on December 4, 2013. "Seeing a concept that started out as an idea come to life is like giving birth," I wrote in my first ever post on the site. "I can't wait to see my baby grow, but more so, I'm looking forward to seeing how she touches the lives of all those she comes in contact with." As I read that now, a flood of emotions comes over me because we've provided greater visibility of Afro-Latinxs, which is beautiful to see, but there's also still a great deal of work to do, particularly in amplifying the stories of Black Latinxs living in Latin America.

In my seven-year journey building *Ain't I Latina?*, I've learned so much about telling our stories with care, the limits of visibility, and the media's reaction to the Afro-Latinx-centered conversations online, as well as my positionality and my views on terms like Afro-Latina/o/x. In journalism school, we are taught that true journalists must remain objective, removed from the interview subjects. I quickly learned that in order to really tell Black diasporic stories with nuance, there's no such thing as objectivity. When you can relate to the anger, pain, disappointment, shame—what will an objective, removed stance provide for the story, and more importantly, the person on the other side of the recorder? Affirmations like "thank you for seeing us" or "you gave words to my exact experience" remind me that there's no blueprint for this, but trusting the power of an unguarded conversation will capture exactly what's needed.

Over the last decade, I've contributed to Latinx media, so I'm more certain than ever that visibility is not where the conversation ends. Recently, when prominent Latinxs in Hollywood were up in arms about the 2020 Emmy nominations, there was no acknowledgment of Jharrel Jerome, reportedly the first Afro-Latinx to win an acting Emmy for best lead actor in a limited series for his performance in Netflix's *When They See Us*, or Yalitza Aparicio, the first Indigenous woman of Mixtec and Triqui heritage nominated for best actress at the Oscars for her role in *Roma*. Though, in theory, Latinx is meant to be inclusive of many different identities, the calls for greater inclusion and visibility inevitably exclude Black and/or Indigenous Latinxs. The project of Latinidad is an intentional and dangerous one—and the media supports it. Not only does Latinidad erase Blackness and Indigeneity, but it also relies on one's proximity to whiteness, as well as how much privilege one has based on gender, sexual preference, socioeconomic status, immigrant status, language spoken, and mobility, among other things. Those who find themselves closest to what's "socially acceptable" benefit most.

Latinidad/Hispanidad supports white supremacy, and its

harmful history can be traced back to roughly the late 1400s through the trans atlantic slave trade, where a majority of the 10.7 million enslaved that survived the Middle Passage ended up in Central and South America and the Caribbean. As the slave trade progressed and the need to maintain privileges for a select few became apparent, the Spanish unveiled the sistema de castas—a system that determined advancement based on race or racial mixture. The casta's remnants are evident across Latin America today, and within the way US-based Latinxs operate. Even with the use of Latinx/o/a, the umbrella term still upholds an exclusionary foundation.

I've seen this in action my entire life. The constant questions surrounding where my parents were born, which parent is actually from Honduras (as if to see which parent isn't Black), my surname, and which languages I speak are an attempt to erase my existence or validate my identity through a linear view. It's insulting. As a Black woman in the US, it's bad; however, my experiences abroad have hinted at worse, and I know that to be the case from family and friends living in Latin America and the Caribbean.

My lived experience as a Garifuna woman born and raised in the Bronx is different than that of my family in Honduras. I started unpacking my positionality more deeply within the last several years because the reflection calls for radical honesty and a true understanding of the privileges and spaces I occupy. It's made me name all my identities—Black Latina/Afro-Latina, Afro-Indigenous, Black American, Caribbean American, Garifuna, to name a few—when I speak about my experiences. Yes, I'm proud to be Garifuna, but my day-to-day doesn't mirror that of someone who was born and raised Garifuna in Honduras. It's a given that, as a Black person anywhere, you'll have to navigate anti-Blackness and white supremacy and its many byproducts. But from education and employment opportunities to racism and state-sanctioned violence, they experience inequities and navigate oppression in ways I won't ever have to because of my Americanness. Many of us with a hyphenated identity (specifically US-based) have a tendency to claim the country where our roots lie without contextualizing our points of privilege and overall access. The digital space has helped name those nuances. While it challenged me in necessary ways and provided community, the greater visibility around Afro-Latinidad has, ironically, shifted the focus away from racialized Black people.

Again, Blackness in Latin America is not a new conversation, and I'm forever grateful for the elders, ancestors, and peers who've paved the way for Afro-Latinidad to become a more recognized discussion and applied pressure to those who have refused to acknowledge our existence. Within the media, greater visibility looked and felt like we were making strides, and while there were a number of wins on that front—more headlines, an uptick in social media pages centered on Afro-Latinidad, and even greater inclusion in front and behind-the-scenes of scripted and non-scripted shows—I started seeing a shift in the way the term Afro-Latina/o/x was being used. Afro-Latina is a term I've used to center my Blackness, not to say that I'm less Black or "special Black." I take great pride in saying, "I'm Black, period," but the term Afro-Latina seemed to take on a new meaning among those who see it as simply a trend, not an existence that comes with an unquestionable understanding of self and how you're perceived in the world.

The narrative that you find Blackness or can pick and choose when you want to identify as Black began taking center stage, and that doesn't sit well with me. While I'll still use the term in solidarity with other Black Latinxs, Afro-Latina is no longer my preferred choice. I'm a Black woman, Negra, and that's enough. Blackness is not restricted to one locale, so identifying as such doesn't negate my ties to Honduras. However, it does ensure that my Blackness is centered.

My family, particularly the matriarchs, are that reminder for me.

I can only remember bits and pieces of my first visit to Honduras. It was June 1994, and I'd just wrapped up the first grade. Memories of playing between the waves in Iriona Viejo with my older brother and cousins, consuming topoyiyo to beat the heat, meeting my paternal grandparents for the first time in Ciriboya—and the distinct *mon* my grandfather placed at the close of his sentences—and even my failed attempt to take an unhatched egg from under its mother, followed by the sharpest beak hitting my middle finger and the chase around Abuela's kitchen. Her kitchen, separate and diagonal from the house, held a clay oven where she masterfully prepared all meals. She was ecstatic to see my father (her son), mother, and brother again and to meet me for the first time. Hudutu was our treat once we settled in.

Same trip, different memory.

My bisabuela, petite, had a presence about her. Old age took her eyesight, but she didn't miss a beat. Her inner sight was sharper than most people's twenty-twenty vision. If you're wondering what I mean, well, one evening, as the sun began to set, to prevent mosquitoes from overtaking the house, she closed the door. It was getting dark, so I decided we should crack the door for more light. I mean, who did I think I was in somebody else's home, let alone my great-grandmother's? She closed it. I cracked it again. She, without question, closed it. She didn't reprimand me or utter a word. She intrigued me. I'd never get to sit with her again, but she lives on in my abuelita, my mom, my aunts, in me.

Whether earthside or not, my grandmothers and all the women in my lineage have played a part in the person I've become. Their gifts to me include:

Ancestral memory, unexplainable connections made that are too coincidental to pinpoint.

Courage, to speak our many truths.

Lineage, the understanding that we've been and will always be.

Love, of self and our people. Garinagu wagia, súwan dán.

Oral traditions, that exist in our recipes, healing modalities, our stories, our native tongue.

Survival, for the times past, present, and future that
   we've made it through.

These are their greatest gifts to me. And, just as they
did, I will pass them on—and then some—to those who
come after.

A Mi Orden
A MEDITATION ON DICHOS
Elizabeth Acevedo

My grandfather, a man who worked with oxen his whole
life, who had a patrón & specific duty in maintaining other
people's crops, came to the United States when I was five
years old. He was the first person my mother brought
over with her papers. & this man donned in a fedora hat,
& high-waist slacks, & the smooth guayabera shirt iconic
of a man of his age would grab my little hand, tie on my
high-top Reeboks & would walk me to & from preschool
every single day. I vividly remember how he would hold
the school door open for me & answer my quiet thank-
you with a kindly uttered, "A tu orden."

A tu orden. I've always loved that phrase. It was so
awfully courteous of Papá, granting a five-year-old such
gallantry. I'm sure I giggled & repeated it back to him &
then proceeded to adopt that phrase as my own. My up-
rooting "de nada" from my vernacular & repotting "a tu
orden" is directly linked to my innate fascination with language & with my desire to make other people feel what

my grandfather made me feel with his response: respected, powerful.

But recently, as I've begun to look back at the shiniest Spanish phrases directed at me as a child, coupled with the very common Dominican expectations dangled above my head, I've started to sense that, connected, they were a constellation heavily riddled with subtly teaching me my place.

For example, I think of the oft spit epithet: "malcriada." One of the worst things to be: ill-raised, ill-bred. The performance of "being raised" was often simply being obedient. To be raised was the opposite of wild. But there were so many occasions that a bit more wildness would have saved me heartache, would have saved the boldest version of me, period. But I wanted to be read as "biencriada"—a word I just made up—in any & all circumstances.

Another phrase directed at me: "Tú te mandas sola?"

It most often happened in public: my mother's heart-shaped mouth sharpening around the reminder. Let's say we were walking down Amsterdam, & my growing & quick legs meant I moved several steps ahead of Mami—behind me, I'd hear that question, Mami's coded way of saying slow down, come back, don't move too far ahead. Or, let's say for a second I got caught up in enthusiasm with a friend & ran to my mother to tell her I was going to go play two stoops over. There's the phrase again: "O, o, pero tu crees que te mandas?" To which I would internally respond with, "No. I guess I am not the boss of me." Or perhaps I would pout or just silently & placidly agree with whichever parent was asking the question that indeed, I had been mistaken in believing this body was one that I governed.

Lately, I have been having a lot more conversations with my mother. Hard, painful conversations that often center on her own upbringing. My maternal grandmother is a tank of a woman, & when my mother was a little girl, she was often steamrolled. Which is to say, my mother made so many efforts to raise me differently. & when I ask her about these little sayings & idioms, when I mention I heard them so many times I internalized them, she could only shake her head. There were so many things she tried to guard my childhood against, but what is a child if not permeable? Things slipped through—especially the phrases we learn to fall back on to understand ourselves in the world. When I tell you my mother worked damn hard to ensure I was safe? I mean it. If that lovely lady could have walked me to school & picked me up all the way through college, I, honest to God, believe she would have. Into my masters, even! & so it's not to disparage my mom or the folks who raised me that I say this, but it does need to be said:

We need repurposed or entirely new language with which to raise. With which to rise.

I'm often asked if my first novel, *The Poet X,* is autobiographical. In fact, I would bet all my chelitos that it's by far the question I get asked the most, & I love to loudly & clearly say, "*The Poet X* is fiction, it is not based on events that actually happened to me, although it did draw from my emotional truths & questions I had when I was a teenager."

That said, there is one scene in the novel that was drawn directly from my life. When I was a junior in high school, I was in a secret "situationship" with a boy who sat next to me in chemistry class. He always had a fresh shape-up, crisp, smudgeless Js, & as was the style back in the early 2000s, way too large white tees. He was half Trinidadian & half Dominican, & when my parents went to bed at night, I would sneak out of my room to message him on the family computer.

I had been told since I was old enough to remember that I was not allowed to have a boyfriend. My parents believed that if I focused on romance, any number of things could befall me: teen pregnancy, dropping out of school, not going to college, joining a gang, disgracing the family, etc. & I tried very hard throughout my youth to respect their wishes, which means I tried hard to never get caught with any of my little boyfriends. But a girl still had a code. & that meant I didn't want to *outright* disrespect my parents & go over to a boy's house, where all kinds of things might happen. Instead, I chose to honor their desire to avoid all of those outcomes they didn't want by doing my dirt publicly. On the train. A full make-out session with this chem partner who was a kind-of sort-of boyfriend.

Turns out my father was in the train car right next to us, his face pressed against the window due to the number of people packed on during rush hour. He couldn't have looked away if he wanted to, & according to him, he wanted to. Enough so that he got off the train a whole stop early.

My raising, & punishments, were often left to my mother. It might be helpful to know, my momma is old school. & so I arrived home to her fuming face.

Despite the many times I'd asked my mother about relationships, or boyfriends, or when I'd be allowed to have one, she'd always respond with when I was an adult. My mother grew up in an old-school way, a time in DR where her own father was able to enforce that any suitors his daughters had first came to the house & met him & that all couple meetings were held in a place under sharp supervision. In other words, a different era & cultural experience than my own courtships out in these Harlem streets. My experiences, like those of my best friend, of Rosita from upstairs, of Silvia from across the hall, of countless girls in our hood who had watched countless other girls bend island rules to first-generation rules & do the same thing: hide as much as you can from your parents. You're doing something wrong, even if it feels good, & your body is not yours. So, don't get caught.

& it's not like I didn't know that a sexual interaction would be an upsetting thing. I remember when I was eight years old, an upstairs neighbor was caught kissing her secret boo in the building's ill-lit staircase & her father's response was terrifying. In front of the whole building, he dragged her out to the street, & his hands were heavy. I learned from observing that interaction the kinds of measures some parents might take to ensure that their expressed & unexpressed mandates were followed. & while my own parents showed more restraint, it is necessary to say that communal expectations & fears are also held up communally. We watch the village, even as the village watches over us. & this exchange teaches what to go toward & what to be afraid of. & many of us were taught the person we should fear most was ourselves. Giving in to ourselves would be dire.

My mother's disappointment in me wasn't violent, but it was palpable. She pointed out that anyone from the neighborhood could have been on that train. She questioned if the reason I wanted to go away to college was to be a ho. She questioned if I should be allowed to go away to college at all. Things fizzled down over the next few weeks, & I was allowed to return to my clubs, & to my after-school activities, & to have my phone back. I was even allowed to apply to & attend college in a different city. If one were to consider the consequences, a stern talking to & loss of privileges for two weeks, it wasn't that deep. But it reinforced so much. My desires & burgeoning sexuality were stifled, implicitly & explicitly; I often wonder how my most tender & subversive emotions survived without any air. It came up in the ways I was taught to tightrope walk the way my family & community valued sexiness, but not sexuality. It was clear in what I wore:

No sheer items

No midriffs

No short shorts

No hint of cleavage (bralessness wasn't even a consideration)

No miniskirts

My ability to express myself, to celebrate my body, had very clear guardrails. & the rules didn't always make sense

to me. One of my favorite pairs of jeans were these pock-
etless pants made by Rocawear with a huge "R" branded
on the right cheek. I loved the way those jeans made my
butt look. I loved how grown I felt in them, how when I
put them on, it was like I was adorned in denim armor.
Strangely enough, my mother loved those jeans on me too.
& it's this kind of duality, the push & pull my own parents must have felt in regard to a ruled body, that makes
me wonder if the issue wasn't only in my parents' beliefs
around my body & my agency, but also in the ways they
were raised to parrot certain strictures without ever interrogating them. & when faced with interrogation due to the
double standard that existed between how I was raised &
my brothers were raised, sometimes they rose to the occasion, & sometimes they fucked up.

When I walked ahead of my mom, she might have
asked, "si yo me mandaba," but she did not yank
me back

When I got caught kissing on the train, my parents
were disappointed & the conversations we had were
rough, but I was not sent to DR. They took my
phone, & I was restricted to school & home only,
but I was unharmed

When I insisted on getting my eyebrows done even
though my mother thought I was too young, she
shook her head & uttered a "gran poder de Dios"
but otherwise told me not to get them too thin.

When I insisted on getting piercings even though my parents hated them

When I applied to travel to Spain, my parents expressed concern for my safety & were largely worried about their child out in a world por allá, to places they'd never seen, but Mami gave me the money she'd raised for a quinceañera to help fund the trip & she signed the permission slips

My parents, my mom especially, fought hard against the learnings she'd had in order to raise me strong, confident, & brave. She confessed to me recently that her own mother complained that she was too soft on me. But my mother's memories of her childhood wouldn't allow her to pursue the same kind of discipline my grandmother had.

My parents lived in the same apartment for forty-one years. Mainly because my father didn't want to move, despite the tight living quarters. Recently, they've decided to get a larger apartment. It was of my mother's volition at seventy years old to upend what was comfortable for what was possible. & it was after a conversation where I asked her when she was going to stop being the martyr. After seventy years, didn't it make sense to put herself & her desires first, for once? Mami has always told me she doesn't feel her age. She feels like a girl at heart. When put that way, & knowing how my mother has known girls to be raised, it makes sense she does not let herself think of her needs before all the people she loves. That means that Mami loves herself last.

Many of the hurts I have endured in my life stem from an inability to believe I had the right to ask for what I needed & to stop others from doing to me what they wanted. So much of my life has been spent looking for permission, for outside validation, but together, individually, & with a therapist, Mami & I are both unraveling old phrases into new modes of being.

& this is why I chose to write this particular essay, for this particular moment: I do not want any more girls growing up & waiting until they are in their thirties to start having conversations about their agency, how they are ALWAYS able to say what does or does not make them comfortable, & to start interrogating the language used in their direction that might not serve them. Teen Latinas have been steadily one of the fastest-growing groups exhibiting suicide ideation & committing self-harm.

So many young Latinas struggle privately & inwardly with being overwhelmed, depressed, & anxious, & those feelings are met with the external expectations of boca cerrada te ves más bonita. We ask our girls to split themselves into accommodating pieces & then wonder at how thoroughly they've splintered. If our wounds do not have a witness, if they do not have a voice, the bleeding still happens. Internal bleeding is as dangerous as any open cut.

I am working really hard to remember, that this life?

This very one I'm out here living? It is ruled by only one person. & I give myself the thanks. & whenever I give thanks, I also reply: It's on my orders, love. This whole big messy life. A mi orden.

About the Authors

Mark Oshiro is the author of the young adult novels *Anger Is a Gift*, winner of the 2019 Schneider Family Book Award, *Each of Us a Desert*, and the middle-grade novel *The Insiders*. When they are not writing or traveling, Mark is busy trying to fulfill their lifelong goal: to pet every dog in the world.

Naima Coster is the author of two novels, *What's Mine and Yours* and *Halsey Street*, a finalist for the 2018 Kirkus Prize for Fiction. In 2020, she received the National Book Foundation's "5 Under 35" honor. Naima's stories and essays have appeared in the *New York Times*, *Kweli*, *The Paris Review Daily*, *The Cut*, *Catapult*, *The Rumpus*, and elsewhere. She has taught writing for over a decade in community settings, youth programs, and universities. She lives in Brooklyn with her family.

Natasha Diaz is a born and raised New Yorker, currently residing in Brooklyn. Both an author and screenwriter, her work has placed as a quarterfinalist in the Austin Film Festival and a finalist for both the NALIP Diverse Women in Media Initiative and the Sundance Episodic Story Lab. Her essays can be found in *The Establishment* and *Huff-Post*. Natasha's first novel, *Color Me In*, was a finalist for the National Jewish Book Award.

Meg Medina is an award-winning and *New York Times* best-selling author who writes picture books as well as middle grade and young adult fiction. Her titles include *Merci Suárez Changes Gears*, a Newbery Medal winner; *Burn Baby Burn*, long-listed for the National Book Award, short-listed for the Kirkus Prize, and a finalist for the *Los Angeles Times* Book Prize; and *Yaqui Delgado Wants to Kick Your Ass*, winner of the 2014 Pura Belpré Award. When she's not writing, Meg works on community projects that support girls, Latino youth, and/or literacy. She serves on the National Board of Advisors for the Society of Children's Book Writers and Illustrators and is a faculty member of Hamline University's Masters of Fine Arts in Children's Literature. She lives with her family in Richmond, Virginia.

Julian Randall is a Living Queer Black poet from Chicago. Their poetry and essays are published in *The New York Times Magazine*, *Poetry*, and *Vibe*. They are the recipient of a Pushcart Prize. They hold an MFA in poetry from Ole Miss. Their first book, *Refuse*, won the Cave Canem Poetry Prize and was a finalist for an NAACP Image Award. Julian has previously worked as a youth mentor, teaching writing workshops to children on house arrest.

Pilar Ramirez and the Prison of Zafa is their debut children's novel.

Saraciea J. Fennell is a Black Honduran writer, and the founder of The Bronx Is Reading. She is also a book publicist who has worked with many award-winning and *New York Times* bestselling authors. Fennell is board chair of Latinx in Publishing, on the advisory board of People of Color in Publishing, and the creator of Honduran Garifuna Writers. She lives in the Bronx with her family and poodle, Oreo.

Ibi Zoboi is the *New York Times* bestselling author of the middle grade novel *My Life as an Ice Cream Sandwich* and the young adult novels *American Street*, a National Book Award finalist, and *Pride.* She is also the coauthor of *Punching the Air* with prison reform activist Dr. Yusef Salaam of the Exonerated Five and editor of *Black Enough: Stories of Being Young & Black in America.* Ibi holds an MFA in Writing for Children & Young Adults from Vermont College of Fine Arts. Her writing has been published in *The New York Times Book Review, The Horn Book Magazine,* and *The Rumpus,* among others. As an educator, she is the recipient of several grants from the Brooklyn Arts Council for her community-based programs for teen girls in both Brooklyn and Haiti. She's worked for arts organizations such as Teachers & Writers Collaborative and Community Word Project as a writer in residence and teaching artist in New York City public schools. Born in Port-au-Prince, Haiti, and raised in New York City, Ibi now lives in Maplewood, New Jersey, with her husband and their three children.

Cristina Arreola is a writer and reader based in New York City. Currently working in marketing and publicity for a book publisher, Cristina is formerly the books editor at *Bustle.* She is a graduate of the Medill School of Journalism at Northwestern University and a loud and passionate advocate of books.

Kahlil Haywood is a writer, editor, and content creator from Brooklyn, New York. Prideful about his candor, Kahlil started his blog *Damn, He Got A Point* as an undergrad in 2009. A column with its namesake began in 2010 for the Long Island University Post *Pioneer* newspaper. Haywood's content chronicles the experiences of a millennial Afro-Latino man. His work discusses politics, dating, and contemporary culture. The art, and the content, is all created to elicit discussion and promote further understanding. Haywood's talents have been shared with sites such as *Single Black Male, Bossip,* and *Madame Noire.* He loves the bar "I'm not a biter, I'm a writer for myself and others," as he believes it best describes the spirit in which he expresses himself. Haywood currently works as a social media editor for the *Daily Mail* and as a columnist for *Ebony.* He continues to be more inspired than ever to create thoughtful and meaningful content.

Zakiya N. Jamal was born in Queens, raised on Long Island, and currently resides in Brooklyn. In other words, she's a

New Yorker through and through. She holds a BA in English from Georgetown University and an MFA in Creative Writing with a concentration in Writing for Children and Young Adults from The New School. She currently works at Scholastic as the trade social media manager and has been published in *Romper, BuzzFeed, People.com, Thought Catalog,* and more.

Lilliam Rivera is an award-winning writer and author of children's books. Her books include the middle-grade novel *Goldie Vance: The Hotel Whodunit* and young adult novels *Dealing in Dreams, The Education of Margot Sanchez,* and the Pura Belpré Honor Book *Never Look Back.* Her work has also appeared in *The Washington Post, The New York Times,* and *Elle.* Lilliam lives in Los Angeles.

Jasminne Mendez is a Dominican-American poet, educator, playwright, and award-winning author. Mendez has had poetry and essays published by or forthcoming in *New England Review, Kenyon Review, Gulf Coast, The Rumpus,* and others. She is the author of *Island of Dreams,* which won an International Latino Book Award, and *Night-Blooming Jasmin(n)e: Personal Essays and Poetry. A Bucket of Dirty Water: Memories of My Girlhood* and *Josefina's Habichuelas* will be released in 2021. Her first full poetry collection, *Machete,* will be released in 2022. She is an MFA graduate of the creative writing program at the Rainier Writing Workshop at Pacific Lutheran University and a University of Houston alum.

Ingrid Rojas Contreras is the author of *Fruit of the Drunken Tree*, a silver medal winner in First Fiction from the California Book Awards. Her writing has appeared in *The New York Times Magazine*, *The Cut*, *The Believer*, and elsewhere. A new work of nonfiction, a family memoir about her grandfather, a curandero from Colombia who it was said had the power to move clouds, is forthcoming in 2022.

Janel Martinez is a Bronx-raised writer and founder of the award-winning blog *Ain't I Latina?*, an online destination celebrating Afro-Latinx womanhood. She's appeared as a featured guest on national shows and outlets, such as *BuzzFeed*, *Essence*, NPR, and Sirius XM, and her work has appeared in *Adweek*, Univision Communications, *O, the Oprah Magazine*, Remezcla, and *The New York Times*. She received the Afro-Latino Festival of New York's Digital Empowerment Award and was recognized at City Hall by the New York City Council; the Black, Latino, and Asian Caucus; and the Bronx Delegation to the NYC Council for her contributions as a woman of Garifuna descent.

Elizabeth Acevedo is the *New York Times* bestselling author of *The Poet X*, *With the Fire on High*, and *Clap When You Land*. Her critically acclaimed debut novel, *The Poet X*, won the 2018 National Book Award for Young People's Literature. She is also the recipient of the Printz Award for Excellence in Young Adult Fiction, the CILIP Carnegie Medal, and the Boston Globe–Horn Book Award.

Additionally, she was honored with the 2019 Pure Belpré Award for celebrating, affirming, and portraying Latinx culture and experience. She holds a BA in performing arts from The George Washington University and an MFA in creative writing from the University of Maryland. Acevedo has been a fellow of Cave Canem, Cantomundo, and a participant in the Callaloo Writer's Workshops. She is a National Poetry Slam Champion and resides in Washington, DC, with her love.

Acknowledgments

Where do I even begin? So many people have supported me along this journey, but I would be nowhere without having my friend and agent, Patrice Caldwell, who put my feet to the fire to get this anthology together, so thank you a million times over. Thank you to my family who have and continue to encourage me to keep writing and to do all the fiftyeleven things that I do! To my husband, who has been a rock throughout this process, thank you for taking care of me, making sure I eat, but most important, reminding me to take breaks and have snuggle time—I love you and appreciate all that you do for me and the family! Special thanks to my mini-me, Azariah, who makes me laugh and always knows the right thing to say when I'm stuck. Thank you for reminding me that life brings us joy and sometimes we must take a second to enjoy it together. Thank you to my mom and stepdad for never giving up on me and constantly shouting about me to anyone who will listen. I'm pretty sure folks are tired of hearing about your daughter's accomplishments, ha!

Ebony LaDelle, my ace, thank you for your support, your friendship, and for answering my frantic text messages at odd hours. Isa Caban and Anthony Parisi, thank you for always allowing me to lean on you and for your unwavering support. Thank you to my best friends Maegan Grayson Hill and Mechell Turner, for being all-around awesome, and for making sure I didn't you know, lose my head editing this book while also planning a wedding!

Thank you to everyone at Flatiron! From that initial meeting y'all blew me away, it was the most thoughtful publishing meeting I have ever witnessed, and not to mention how Bob Miller just casually dropped in to say hello. ☺ I am so, so, so thankful and thrilled that y'all saw something special in this anthology. Sarah Barley and Caroline Bleeke, where would I even be without your thoughtful feedback and insight? This editorial experience has been amazing and I'm so happy I get to work with you both! Sydney Jeon, Jordan Forney, Amelia Possanza, Nikkia Rivera, Nancy Trypuc, you are all masterminds, publicity and marketing gold, and most important, dream makers—thank you for all that you do, and will continue to do to get this book into the hands of readers. Special thanks to all the wonderful folks at Flatiron/Macmillan who have touched this anthology and championed me and the contributors: Megan Lynch, Bob Miller, Cristina Gilbert, Malati Chavali, Erin Gordon, Keith Hayes, Kelly Gatesman, Nneka Bennett, Michelle McMillian, Melanie Sanders, Jason Reigal, Emily Walters, Megan Kiddoo, Jennifer Edwards, Jess Brigman, Talia Sherer, Peter Janssen, Bryon Echeverria, Alexandra Quill, Talia Sherer, Emily Day, Mary Beth Roche, Matie Argiropoulos, Robert Allen, Amber Cortes, and Emily Dyer.

Thank you to all the folks at Howard Morhaim Literary Agency and New Leaf Literary & Media. Meredith Barnes, thank you for all the advice, answering my questions, and your overall guidance. Shout out to all the writers who have shared advice and allowed me to take up space and write alongside you at retreats: Tiffany D. Jackson, Ashley Woodfolk, Kwame Mbalia, Mark Oshiro, Jalissa Corrie, Justin A. Reynolds, Zoraida Cordova, and all of my Honduran and Garifuna Writers crew!

Last but certainly not least, thank you to all the wonderful contributors. Like wow, I still can't believe I got to edit you! Thank you for being part of this collection; I am honored to have worked with you. To the readers who have picked up and supported this work, thank you, we write for you!

PLEASE NOTE: In order to provide reading groups with the most informed and thought-provoking questions possible, it is necessary to reveal important aspects of the plot of this novel—as well as the ending. If you have not finished reading *Wild Tongues Can't Be Tamed* by Saraciea J. Fennell, we respectfully suggest that you may want to wait before reviewing this guide.

Wild Tongues Can't Be Tamed
DISCUSSION QUESTIONS

1. In her introduction, Saraciea J. Fennell writes of the contributors, "We are letting our truths run wild, and pushing against whatever it is you think is the ideal Latinx individual." The anthology celebrates the diversity of the Latinx diaspora and the full range of identities among the contributors. Are there also common stereotypes and preconceptions that the contributors face and interrogate?

2. Mark Oshiro understands the phrase "eres un pocho" to mean "You gave up your culture. You assimilated . . . You betrayed who you were." What pressures do they face to assimilate, and what are the consequences of assimilation? How do they eventually begin to push back against assimilation to reclaim their full identity?

3. In "The Price of Admission," Naima Coster writes, "I often think about what we lose when we deny the complexity of our stories, our families, and ourselves in service of some victorious narrative—the desire to declare ourselves triumphant, worthy, palatable to whiteness. I think about the testimonies and self-expression we lose, as well as the opportunities to accept ourselves and connect to one another." What does she mean? How does her piece acknowledge and embrace some of that complexity, through her relationship with her father-in-law? How can writing be, as she describes it, "a way to move away from shame"?

4. Why is Tío Francisco so important to Meg Medina growing up, in "The Mark of a Good Man"? How does he, like Naima Coster's father-in-law, complicate our understanding of what a "good man" or "good immigrant" is? Why are those terms problematic?

5. What do you think Natasha Díaz means by the phrase "caution song" in her poem? How do her closing lines—"if you call me spicy, / you should expect me to bite your tongue"—resonate with the anthology's title, *Wild Tongues Can't Be Tamed*?

6. In "#Julian4SpiderMan," Julian Randall writes, "The consequence of being seen is that you're seen." What do they mean? How does this sentiment resonate throughout both their piece and the anthology as a whole?

7. Multiple contributors describe the experience of being asked, "What are you?" What does that phrase mean, and why is it hurtful?

8. In "Half In, Half Out," Saraciea J. Fennell writes, "I desperately needed to know what our roots were so I could dictate my identity—not other people." Similarly, Zakiya N. Jamal writes in "Cuban Impostor Syndrome," "As long as I know where I come from, I know exactly who I am." What is the importance of uncovering and understanding family history for these writers?

9. Several contributors address the label "Afro-Latinx" in their pieces. For some, like Julian Randall, it's a powerful way to claim their full identity, while for others, like Ibi Zoboi and Janel Martinez, it doesn't feel like enough. Discuss what "Afro-Latinx" means and why it's so complicated. How does colorism operate within the Latinx diaspora, as we see in this anthology?

10. Cristina Arreola struggles to claim her Mexican-American identity in "The Land, the Ghosts, and Me": "Away from home, I began to feel that I hadn't been steeped in the culture long enough to make me strong with its flavor, but just enough that you couldn't hide the scent." Similarly, Zakiya N. Jamal describes her "Cuban Impostor Syndrome" and not feeling like she "fit the mold of what a Cuban should be." How do these writers' experiences compare and contrast? How are they able, over the course of their essays, to claim their full Latinx identities?

11. Both Kahlil Haywood in "Paraíso Negro" and Janel Martinez in "Abuela's Greatest Gift" describe traveling to Central America to visit family in Panama and Honduras, respectively. How do those

trips deepen their understanding of their own identities? What insights do they share about the differences and similarities between the Latinx experience in the US and Central America? Do you agree with Kahlil that "once you increase travel and meet all of the people, you have no choice but to have a more varied view of the world"?

12. Why is theater so important and liberating for Jasminne Mendez in "Alaiyo" when she first discovers it in middle school? Why does she ultimately stop performing onstage and turn to poetry and spoken word instead?

13. One of the major cultural differences between Ingrid Rojas Contreras's Colombian family and her husband's white American family is how they deal with conflict. In "Invisible," she writes of her in-laws, "being conflict-averse meant that they all chose to avert their eyes away from things that might invite discord. They could not see, and I could not get any of them to understand, however hard I tried, that discord can, in turn, invite justice." What does she mean? Do you agree?

14. Some of the contributors in this anthology describe growing up fluent in Spanish, while others never learned or don't know it well. Why is the Spanish language often so fraught within the Latinx community? How can it be both empowering and exclusionary?

15. In "A Mi Orden," Elizabeth Acevedo writes, "internal bleeding is as dangerous as any open cut." What does she mean? How does that line resonate with Lilliam Rivera's experience, described in "More Than Nervios," with her own mental health struggles? What do these two essays suggest about the importance of speaking up and asking for help, as well as the difficulty of doing so, especially as a Latina?

16. Was there a piece in the anthology that particularly moved you or surprised you? If so, which one and why?